William Henry Harrison Murray

John Norton's Thanksgiving party

And other stories

William Henry Harrison Murray

John Norton's Thanksgiving party
And other stories

ISBN/EAN: 9783742836762

Manufactured in Europe, USA, Canada, Australia, Japa

Cover: Foto ©Andreas Hilbeck / pixelio.de

Manufactured and distributed by brebook publishing software (www.brebook.com)

William Henry Harrison Murray

John Norton's Thanksgiving party

W. H. H. MURRAY'S WORKS.

ADVENTURES IN THE WILDERNESS, or Camp Life in the Adirondacks.
Illustrated. Cloth, $1.25; paper, 50 cents.

THE STORY THAT THE KEG TOLD ME, and THE MAN WHO DIDN'T KNOW MUCH. Adirondack Tales. Vol. I.
Illustrated. Price, $1.50.

THE MYSTERY OF THE WOODS, and THE MAN WHO MISSED IT. Adirondack Tales. Vol. II.
Illustrated. Price, $1.50.

HOW JOHN NORTON THE TRAPPER KEPT HIS CHRISTMAS.
Small quarto. Illustrated. $1.50.

JOHN NORTON'S THANKSGIVING PARTY, and other Stories.
Illustrated. Price, $1.25.

THE BUSTED EX-TEXAN, and other Stories.
Price, $1.00.

LAKE CHAMPLAIN AND ITS SHORES.
Price, $1.00.

DEACONS.
Illustrated. Price, cloth, 75 cents; paper, 50 cents.

THE GAIN OF DYING.
(Religious Address.) Price, paper, 25 cents.

CONTINENTAL UNITY.
Price, paper, 25 cents.

DAYLIGHT LAND.
Superbly illustrated with 150 engravings, printed in tint, from paintings by J. D. Woodward, C. Broughton, and other artists. Unique paper covers, $2.50; cloth, $3.50; cloth, extra gilt, $4.00.

MAMELONS and UNGAVA.
Two Canadian Idyls. Price, $1.50.

CONES FOR THE CAMP FIRE.
Price, 50 cents.

DE WOLFE, FISKE & CO.
361 and 365 Washington Street, Boston.

JOHN NORTON'S

THANKSGIVING PARTY

AND

OTHER STORIES

BY

W. H. H. MURRAY

BOSTON
DE WOLFE, FISKE & CO.
361 AND 365 WASHINGTON STREET

PREFACE.

WHILE working away at my larger and more pretentious stories these shorter ones have been struck off,—clippings of the chisel as they might be called—which the affectionate partiality of my family has collected and offered to the public. It may be that some may be entertained by the reading of them; if such should prove to be the case I should be pleased.

W. H. H. MURRAY.

CONTENTS.

	PAGE
John Norton's Thanksgiving Party	9
Henry Herbert's Thanksgiving	38
A Strange Visitor	62
The Shadow on the Wall	77
Was it Suicide?	125
The Old Beggar's Dog	142
Who was He?	171

JOHN NORTON'S THANKSGIVING PARTY.

It was November twenty-sixth, and a clearer, brighter day never dawned on the world. The earth was white as snow could make it, and the lake stretched away a smooth plane of dazzling whiteness. Overhead the sky was hard and glistening like the gleaming sides of broken glass suddenly parted by the hammer's stroke. The very sun looked chilly. Its rays were thin and short, as if the frost had attenuated them and shrunk them back into the mother orb; for to them there was no projection, and in the place of a fiery globe there stood in the steel-blue eastern sky a thin collection of glistening light that seemed to shiver and shrivel as it shone. On the dark, rich evergreens the snow hung in great flecks and patches; but here and there, one that stood sheltered from the wind rose upward like a domed column of monumental whiteness.

The maples in their winter garb of cold gray stood without a leaf. The flexile birches rattled their thin twigs and tapering branches as if they were arborous icicles. In all the sky there was no cloud. Earth and firmament had not in them warmth enough to make even a patch of vapor. The air was so crisp and pure that if one shut his eyes and opened them suddenly he could see a thousand colorless stars in the crisp ether. Through this cool, still, crystalline air only one movement of life: a raven flying unusually high drew with steady strokes its jet black line through the gray light, above the great field of glistening snow.

To the north fifty miles. To the south fifty. To the east and west as far, and within the circle of this great sweep of vision not a house, not a man, not a child. Animals? Yes; a bear, a wolf, a panther, a hermit eagle; perhaps a lost hound seeking in vain amid the snows fresh fallen for its homeward trail. No man? Yes, one. His name? John Norton;—John Norton, the Trapper. Where? Standing on the bank that lifts itself twenty feet from the beach at the northern extremity of Long Lake. Standing on the bank, bareheaded, looking out upon the level expanse of gleaming snow, or lifting his eyes toward the chilly-looking sun. Alone? Totally so. Not a man, not a woman, not a child within fifty miles. And thus John Norton stood utterly alone on Thanksgiving morning in the year — well, no matter about the year. And when the sun arose there was not a human being within fifty miles. And when the sun set there was not a human being within fifty miles. And yet the old man had his party that day. So, if you please, take a few moments from the hours of your gayety with the many that are filling the day with noisy cheerfulness, and read my story: *The story of a party without a guest.*

JOHN NORTON'S THANKSGIVING PARTY.

"Thanksgivin' Day, eh?" said John Norton to himself. "Lord-a-massy! how short the years be! It sartinly seems as if the Lord cut 'em off at either eend, and left nothin' but the middle arter a man gits to be fifty. Last year — the same as it was yesterday, — last year, — let me see; where was I last year? Why, sartin! we was trappin'. Yis; he and me was trappin', — he and me." And the old man repeated the words with a peculiarly sweet and solemn tenderness, as if into his mental calculation there had come some reminiscence of affection.

"Yis, we was trappin' last year, — the same as it was yesterday, — and we trudged in from Mount Seward — and a good thirty-mile tramp it was too — jest to be home Thanksgivin' Day, to keep the old custom up. And when we got home, didn't we find the letter from Henry that half-breed Joe had brought in from the settlements, and the pack-basket full of eenamost everything the heart of man could crave, provided he be reasonable in his cravin'; fur there was tea, and powder and bullets, and the leetle tub of butter, — yis, the leetle tub of butter, as if the boy didn't know that the fat of a goose or the taller of a buck, fur that matter, was good enough for mortal man to spread on his cakes. But the boy was always free in his givin', and the things that he put in that pack fur the Lad and me! Sugar-plums, and leetle sweet things shaped like animals; horses and dogs, birds and pigs. Yis, yis, I remember the pigs, all made out of sugar, with their leetle black twisted tails and pink eyes, that would squeak when ye put yer teeth into 'em. Lord-a-massy! how we laughed when half-breed Joe got one into his mouth, and sot his teeth on to it, and the leetle thing squeaked so sharp that it frightened Joe eenamost out of his wits, and the leetle pig came out of his mouth faster than live ones can go into their pen when the pups git arter 'em". And here the old Trapper was fairly convulsed in mirthful memories of the ludicrous scene.

"Yis, this be Thanksgivin' Day, and in the settlements the bells be ringin' and men and wimmin be comin' and goin'. The old folks be waitin' and the young folks be comin', and the cabins will be all lighted to-night. And everything will be merry, as it should be, for the old custom be a good 'un: That once each year the goodness of the Lord be acknowledged in the merry-makin's of the people; that once each year the children shall come to the place where they was born, and the aged look upon the leetle folks and their happiness. And though there be no bells to ring here amid these hills; and though there be no children to come to my cabin; and though neighbors be not actally plenty; yit here be the arth, and here be the sky, and here I be in good health. And the pups be in the cabin; and here be the goodness of the Lord; and the eyes that be big enough to see all, whether they be in the settlements or in the woods, shall see a happy man here this day." And here the old man paused a moment with a look in his face of contentment and finest peace. In a moment his countenance lighted as with a happy thought, and he said, —

"I wonder ef the pups and me can't put our heads together and git up a party! Yis, I will have a party, — a Thanksgivin' party! — but that means a good deal of eatin'. A Thanksgivin' party! That means a good deal of cookin' and fryin' and fixin'. A Thanksgivin' party! That means dressin' up and lookin' yer best; extra benches at the table and somebody on the benches. Yis, yis, I see it might be did. I'll go and talk it over with the pups;" and turning toward the dell in which his log cabin stood, the old man walked with elastic step down the bank with a look on his face in which pleasure and profoundest thought were equally blended.

Whatever were the "pints" that the old Trapper laid before "the pups," we need not fully rehearse. One of the most singular traits which this remarkable man had, was the respect which he always evinced towards the animal kind. Perhaps his thorough acquaintance with the cunning of the wild tenantry of the woods, — of their keen instincts — if not, indeed, reasoning faculties, — which, more than once, had set at successful defiance his own accurate knowledge and shrewd calculation, — had made him appreciate their intelligence beyond what those who had lacked his chance, and perhaps his power of observation, could do. Be this as it may, it was true that either from a sense of humor or some sincere regard — whose sources could not be apprehended by a stranger, — the Trapper never did undertake any — to him — great work, without "talkin' it over with the pups," as he quaintly phrased it. And so, on his return to the cabin, he first proceeded to prepare and eat his breakfast; to which he also helped the dogs as he had himself, — with somewhat limited strictness, — to which the hounds, lacking the forecast of their master's mind as to what was to come, or filled with a stronger sense of duty as to present opportunity, in their peculiar but effective way, demurred.

"No, no, Rover; ye can't have another morsel. Ye needn't lick yer chops in that kind of invitin' way, as ef I didn't understand ye; for I do. I know jest how ye feel, fur I feel jest so myself; and the reason I scrimp ye is the same as why I scrimp myself: from a sense of duty. Yis, pups, from a sense of duty. Not that I conceit it's actlly mentioned in the Bible that a man sha'n't eat as much at breakfast Thanksgivin' Day as any other day; but because it's sort agin reason, considerin' what is to come. And a man that don't consider on Thanksgivin' mornin' what's to come before the day eends, makes a great mistake, ef his stomach is a good 'un and he has any confidence in the cookin'.

"Now," said the old man, as he shoved the table back, which the half-fed dogs followed with eager eyes, "now," said the old man, as he faced his chair around fronting the fireplace, "we'll jest do a leetle plannin'. Here, Rover, you swing round on this side. There, that's right. Here, Sport, ye come up this side, and don't ye look at them victals agin on the table there onless ye want to be reasoned with sort of arnestly; fur we three be in counsel now, and I want yer best advice. Now, I'll give ye the pints of the case, and ye do the listenin'. And two to listen and one to talk is about the right mixture for a council, I conceit; for that makes it mortally sartin that two of the three won't say nothin' foolish, anyway," and the old man chuckled to himself at his own homely wit. In a moment he resumed: —

"Pups, it's Thanksgivin' day. Do ye know what Thanksgivin' Day is, Rover?" and he laid his left hand on the broad front of the old hound's head, who had moved forward sufficiently to rest his long muzzle on the knee of the Trapper. "Yer an old dog, Rover, and I dare say ye do know, fur ye have feasted fourteen seasons with me, — yis, fourteen times has the day come round sence ye was old enough to remember what ye did; and fourteen times have ye and me eat our fill, — and I dare say more than we oughter, — fur a man becomes like a boy in feastin', and eats agin reason. But I doubt, Sport, if ye know what Thanksgivin' Day is, fur ye are young yit, and the young eat without knowin' the reason of their eatin'; but when they git older they sarch out the reasons of their blessings, and so I will tell ye.

"Thanksgivin' Day be a day fur the stomach and fur the heart, too, pups. It's a day when folks eat of the fatness of the arth; but ye eat with remembrance, and ye eat it with rejoicin' that ye have been spared in the land of the livin' to eat. Thanksgivin' Day, pups, is not only a day fur eatin', but it's a great day fur lovin', — it's a day when friends come together, — when the young birds come back to the old nests — Rover, do you hear, old dog? — when the leetle birds come back to the old nest, and cuddle in agin jest as they used to when they lived in the nest all the time. It's a day fur old folks, and fur young folks, and fur dogs and horses, and everything the Lord has made; but especially it's a day fur them that be gone. Sport, do ye hear? I say it's a day fur them that be gone; and them who have been gone to come back; and them who stayed at home to welcome 'em back. If a man has children, why, then his children come back. If he has brothers and sisters, his brothers and sisters come back. But if he hasn't no children, pups, and he hasn't no brothers and sisters, what's the man to do then? Do ye hear, old dog? If a man, I say, hasn't no children, and he hasn't no brother and sister, what's he goin' to do on Thanksgivin' Day, then?"

The hound, of course, said nothing — at least, not in words — for from him his Maker had withheld the gift of articulate utterance; but some subtle sense had enabled him, perhaps, to interpret both the quaint humor and the quaint pathos of his master's speech, and enabled him to answer the interrogation satisfactorily at least to the mind of the Trapper, for, as the old man closed his interrogation " What shall he do then, old dog? " the dog, who was sitting on his haunches with his muzzle resting on his master's knee, swept the floor with a joyful sweep of his tail, and lifted his eyes to the face of the Trapper with a suggestion of sympathy in their depth which the old Trapper interpreted thus: —

" Ay, ay, I understand ye, pup. If he hasn't got no children, and he hasn't got no brother and sister to come back to see him and make his heart happy, then some friend must come back and see him. Some comrade, or some one who has been a comrade. Some one who has slept with him and eat with him, and shot and trapped with him. Do ye hear, Sport? If he hasn't no children nor brother nor sister, then he must have some comrade — some comrade that's been gone. Do ye hear, pup? I said some comrade that's been gone must come back and keep Thanksgivin' with him." And here the old man paused, looking first at one dog and then at the other; while the two hounds, without moving an eyelid, looked steadfastly, and, as it seemed, sympathetically, into his face.

"Now," said the old man, after a moment's silence, "now, pups, the pints in this case be these: I be a man without wife, without child, without mother or father, without brother or sister. And I have no one of my kith or kin to come and keep Thanksgivin' with me, and the day is likely to be lonesome. I have sometimes thought, pups," continued he slowly, in a tone in which calculation and pathos were mingled, "that perhaps it would have been better ef I'd taken a wife, and not been childless in my old age. Better to have married and settled down in the settlements, and had a frame house for a home, and growed up a family, and had a meetin'-house funeral when the time of my burial had come. But when I conceit what I should have lost that Natur' has gin to me; when I think how ignorant I should have been techin' her ways; how worried I should have been with the manners and habits of the settlements, and how much of happiness I've had in the woods, I can't say that ef I could live it all over agin I'd not leave it all the same way as it is."

All day the Trapper was busy making preparations for the feast. The earnestness with which he threw himself into his labors, and the honesty with which he discussed the merits of the different dishes, would have caused no little amusement to one who could have seen his activity and heard his remarks.

With meats his larder was well stored. From its capacious depths he took first a whole saddle of venison, fairly white with its covering of snowy fat, and deposited it on the huge table that stood in the middle of the room. This he prepared to roast by basting it in front of the fire, which roared and crackled in a huge stone fireplace of at least seven feet front. After he had deposited the venison on the table, he stood gazing at it for a moment, noting with critical and pleased expression the excellence of its condition; and then, after a moment's inspection, a soberer light came into his eyes, and he said to himself, —

"How the boy will like it!"

Next, a wild goose, the last of the southern flight, which had lingered foolishly behind his mates, and which, flying low one morning, had run against the Trapper's bullet, was laid beside the venison. A brace of partridge, a couple of ducks, a monstrous trout, already stuffed for baking, in swift succession were brought out and laid upon the table. Then from the cellar he brought a dozen of potatoes, smooth skinned but small in size, suggestive of piney soil and scant nourishment in growth. A pan of cornmeal and a half bucket of flour; some tea in a little canister; a half pound or so of sugar in a wooden box, whose lid was tied tightly on with a string; two turnips, found in a deserted hunter's camp, and treasured for a great occasion; a bark pail full of wild honey, yellow as amber; some hickory-nuts and some beech-nuts.

This seemed to exhaust the contents of the cupboard; for, after these had been fetched forth, a long search, in which the Trapper thrust his hand into every corner of the dim recess, failed to bring anything else to light but two small bottles, one marked "rhubarb," the other "peppermint." The old man stood for a moment carefully studying their labels. He held them in his hands critically, as if inwardly debating the possibility of utilizing them. But, finally, yielding to some interior decision, prompted, perhaps, by that feeling which is said to be ineradicable in human nature, — a desire to make as good a show of one's possessions as possible, — he deliberately walked to the table and gravely added the two little bottles to the brave show he had spread out for inspection.

"There," said the old man, as he stood complacently contemplating the exhibition before him, "that sartinly looks a good deal like Thanksgivin'. The venison be good. I sartinly thought when I seed him coming down the runway that I never sot my eyes on a fatter buck. The partridges are as fat as natur' allows. The goose was a fool, and when I sighted on her I thought of the boy, and how he would enjoy the taste of her meat. I sartinly can't say much for the 'taters; but considerin' the sile they grow'd in, perhaps they desarve as much credit as the bigger ones in the settlements. The tea is the best of its kind, — so Henry said, — and the boy is sartinly a jedge of the yarb. I can't say much fur the sugar, fur the last time I tasted it I conceited there was a leetle too much grit in it fur honest sweetenin'. But the half-breed who peddled it to me swore it wasn't more than half sand, and it may be the vagabond spoke the truth. The honey is pure as bee ever put into a holler maple. Lord! how well I remember the day the Lad plugged the hole! The medicine may be strong; but I'm no jedge of the stuff, and it may be I was weak in bringin' it out; but the day must be honored, and the leetle bottles sartinly look well on the table. Now, pups, let us git at the cookin'. The days be short; and we shall be hungry afore it's done."

It was evening before the feast was fully prepared. Hour after hour the old man had kept at his work of love with as happy and cheerful a mien as if the coming of night was sure to bring him the presence of those who were far away, — one, in his distant city home; the other, in that home which, whether distant or nigh, we know not, — only knowing it is invisible.

With a taste and skill that would have done credit to the eye and the hand of a woman, the old Trapper, with evergreens and running vines which he had gathered beneath the snow, had trimmed and festooned the interior of his cabin. He had swept and scrubbed the floor until the whitewood boards with which it was laid were as white as the stainless fibre would allow. He had dressed himself in his best suit, — a pair of buckskin breeches tanned with his own hands, a hunting shirt of navy blue, a gift from Herbert; while around his neck was a large cravat of similar color, which the Lad had brought him on his return from a trip he had made to the settlements to sell the result of their joint trapping. His hair he had combed with much care, and, as he stood in front of the great fireplace in the full light of the blazing fire, he presented a picture of such beauty and dignity as we associate with manly strength when age has prepared us to contemplate it with reverence and affection.

For a few moments he stood with a look on his countenance which suggested how distant the mind can be from the body. For it was evident from his expression that his mind was far away from the cabin in which he stood; far away from the wilderness with its frozen lakes, its snow-clad mountains, its uninhabited spaces, over whose solitude the day dedicated to companionship had shone but coldly and hurried its decline, as if, repelled by the loneliness, it had hastened to other and more companionable localities.

For a few moments he thus stood; and then with a half-start he roused himself from his revery; and as he started towards the great broad hearthstone on which the now thoroughly cooked repast lay ranged in a row within a foot of the warm ashes, smoking hot, he muttered, —

"I sartinly thought I heerd the bells ring."

It must not be supposed that he said this sadly, for he did not; and yet you must confess, gentle reader, that something of pathos mingles with the quaintness of the position: for here was a man — a companionable man — who, on the day dedicated to human association, and yearning in his heart for human companionship, stood on the hearthstone of his cabin utterly alone; and who, nevertheless, with the purest motive and most heroic determination, was doing the best he might to feed with a sweet delusion the hunger of his heart, hungering for the greeting of love that was not there to greet him.

"Yis," said the old man, as he stooped to lift the haunch of venison, "I sartinly thought I heerd the bells ring. Lord-a-massy! what heft there is to this saddle! There be only one place in which a man can carry sech a piece of meat easily. It is sartinly strange that what seems heavy on the outside of a man actally seems to lift him when he has put it inside. What a strange cretur man is! The heavier he gits the lighter he feels, and the lighter he gits the heavier he feels."

And so talking to himself in a half-humorous fashion, he continued to lift dish after dish upon the table, until the board was actually covered with the smoking viands. Singular that a man, alien to the refinements of society, and especially of woman's society, should have had so fine a sense of the tasteful in him; for into the venison haunch he had stuck little sprigs of the tasselled pine; and one who observed closely the somewhat rude tracery would have noted that the letter "H" stood in green outline against the brown surface of the nicely cooked meat. A bunch of checkerberries drooped from the breast of the partridges, which with deft skill the old Trapper had cooked in such a manner as not to weaken their anatomy, and propped on either side the two birds stood upright on the platter as if alive.

On the plump, fat breast of the goose, in little miniature cones, he had marked the letter "*L.*" The borders of the table were trimmed with green vines. A shrub of oak, to whose twigs the hardy leaves still clung, — leaves that still retained much of their October glory, — stood in the centre of the table, furnishing, as the firelight played on their sheeny surface, an ornamental centre-piece of no mean beauty.

On the table were four plates. At one the hunting-knife of the Trapper was laid, with a stout iron fork and a heavy drinking-cup of solid silver, picked from a battle-field in his earlier days. Beside the other plates were also knives and forks and a cup from which to drink.

The old man contemplated the table for a moment, running his eye over the dishes, as does a housewife the moment before the company is to be seated, to assure herself that all is in order; and, as if satisfied, he said, —

"Three plates fur them that be here, and one fur the stranger that may come. Sartinly, Henry be right; every table should have one plate beyond the family need, — 'a stranger's plate,' as he used to call it. Yis, it's all right:

three plates fur the three that be here, and one fur a stranger, if a stranger should come."

Again the old man stood for a moment looking at the table; and then his face lightened, — lightened with a light so fine and sweet, so gladsome and bright, that his countenance fairly glowed.

He stepped to the wall against which his bed stood; and had you been there in the cabin, and had your eye followed his movements, you would have noticed before his hand touched them, that on the wall over the bell hung two pictures, or, rather, one picture and two frames. For one frame had a picture in it, while the other was empty. Yet the two frames hung side by side, and around them both the old Trapper had woven a border of fadeless vine. The picture that was in the one frame was Herbert's, clad in hunting garb, standing erect with his rifle in his hand, and his paddle lying at his feet. The frame that had no picture in it was not empty to the eye of the Trapper; for, within its borders to his gaze was a face, a simple face, — a face that had no comeliness: a face that none would desire, but which the Trapper had seen take a heavenly beauty amid flame and smoke, and which he and Herbert, while the tears of hundreds fell fast around, had laid in its grave under the pine by the far distant sea.

The old man took the frame with the picture and the frame without a picture from the wall; and, after looking at Herbert's face long and steadily, he hung it on the back of the chair which stood in front of his own at the table, in such a way that the picture's face looked directly into his: and then he went to the chair on his right, and hung the empty frame to it. Again he went to the head of the table, and again looked at the chair at his right, with the poor empty frame hanging to it, and then at the chair in front, from whose back the pictured face of Herbert looked directly into his, and then at the stranger's chair at his left, and said, —

"Yis; three plates fur the three that be here, and one fur the stranger that may come."

Still he hesitated. He half seated himself, and rose again as if in doubt; but at length he said, "Sartinly, it will help." So saying, he stepped to a chest, lifted the lid, and from its depths, in the most gentle manner, he took two bundles, and closing the chest placed them on it as gently, and then, with careful fingers, undid the packages. From the one he took a silver horn, which he placed on the plate in front of Herbert's picture. Then he uncovered the other package, and from it took a violin, and the violin he placed gently down, with the long bow crossed upon it, on the plate in front of the empty frame. And then he stood again a moment by his own chair; and looking at the plate with the violin on it, and then at the plate with the silver horn, and then at the plate at his left, he said, " Yis ; three plates for the three that be here, and a plate for the stranger that may come."

As touching as the circumstances may seem to the reader, the Trapper's nature was of too manly, and, we may say, of too cheerful and humorous a character to be oppressed by what might have been to a weaker nature overpoweringly saddening. For it must be confessed that the old man's attempt " to honor the day," as he put it, and " keep the old custom up," was actually heroic, and persisted in, in the face of obstacles which would have appalled many, even of most cheerful disposition.

In the depth of the wilderness, in the loneliness of his solitary cabin, with mementos that suggested the absence and not the presence of the loved, he was not only endeavoring to keep alive the spirit, but the mannerism of companionship, and succeeding too. For after a survey of the table, and one more glance at the three plates, he seated himself in the chair, and attacked the smoking viands with a countenance not merely cheerful, but which in the relaxations of its lines threatened to break in hilarity.

"I tell ye, Henry," said the old man, addressing not only his words but even his looks to the chair in front of him, as if something more than the pictured face of Herbert filled the empty seat, "I tell ye, Henry, that's the best buck that ever growed. I know where this fat comes from, fur I watched him in his feedin' fur a month; and the roots that he eat was of the sweetest. Yis, I seed his ribs thicken day arter day, and I seed that the day and the condition of the meat would fit each other, and I knowed the Lord had appinted him fur my eatin.' Ye needn't make any reply, boy; fur yer mouth is full of the juices, and time is precious to a mortal when his stomach is empty, and his mouth be filled with venison. Here, Rover, take a piece. I trust ye are sartinly thankful, pup, for the size of yer mouth. There be times when a man's mouth is too big, and there be times when it isn't big enough, and the same holds good with a dog. Open yer mouth wide now, fur I'm goin' to fill it, ef it takes the biggest part of the saddle."

For a moment the old man addressed himself to his plate, when suddenly he stopped and began to laugh, — a laugh which grew as it proceeded, until it rolled out from his ample chest hearty and strong. The cause of his merriment was not revealed until he stuck his fork into one of the diminutive potatoes, which he held up in front of him, and said, —

"Yis, I can jest see ye; that is, I think I can see ye. Lord! what a time ye must have had in growin'! Growin'? ye never growed; ye only started to grow, and ye sartinly must have stopped before ye fairly got started. Here, Rover, open yer mouth."

The hound obeyed. His cavernous jaws came open to their widest stretch. The old man dropped the little morsel into it, and the hound shut his mouth.

"Pup," said the Trapper, "there's a tater somewhere about ye; can ye find it?" The dog never moved a muscle. The morsel had entered his mouth, and glided downward without effort of the organs. To the dog the question as to where it had gone was a conundrum. The only answer he made his master was a silly, mystified look in his eyes, and an interrogative movement of his tail. The question could not be answered.

And so the feast went on. It was eaten with leisure and with heartiness. To every plate with which he helped himself, he helped the dogs even more bountifully. In the midst of his eating he talked with Herbert and the Lad as if they were indeed present. The strong imagination of the man had fairly mastered the occasion. For the time being his friends were with him. Once in his happy self-delusion he even filled the plate appointed for the stranger, as if the hospitality which the humanity of his heart suggested had received a providential recipient.

Thus the volume of the feast flowed on amid laughter and remark, as if the empty chairs were filled, and the companionship which the day had so potently suggested, and the great loving heart of the man so strongly craved, had been vouchsafed. Only once was the peacefulness of the scene threatened with interruption: prompted by the ample abundance of the board and the liberality of his mood, — exaggerated, perhaps, by the occasion, — the old Trapper had fed the hounds with so free a hand, that to them, if dogs have recollections of the ups and downs of life, it would remain a "red letter" day forever. The climax of his lavish bestowments on his two canine companions was reached when, in humorous recklessness, he actually lifted the whole goose, from whose body only a few slices had been cut, and placed it in the open mouth of Sport.

This was an unfortunate act, and illustrated the saying of the ancients, as applicable to dogs as to men, that "the gods can bestow too liberally." For no sooner had the hound received the extravagant gift, than all generosity touching his mate passed out of his soul. The bristles on his back ridged, his tail took the angriest curve and stiffened, and his eyes that could scarcely look over the swelling bulk of the goose that he held in his mouth glowed with a suspicious and angry flame. The elder dog was not slow to resent the suspicion of his companion, nor to envy him the greatness of the fortune which had come to one who was so utterly unworthy, as he in his own soul felt him to be, to receive it.

He answered the exhibition of his companion with equal intensity. His tail lost the waggery of good-nature and curved angrily upward. His wrath grew along the curvature of his back. His eyes, too, glared. The passion of envy soured in an instant his disposition and transported him with rage. He felt that great injustice had been done himself, and, without waiting to discuss the consequences, or even to consider them, with a howl of anger he launched himself upon the goose as if life itself depended upon its possession. What might have been the result, or what violence against canine equity might have been committed had the direful collision not been checked in its very beginning, will never be known. The Trapper brought his foot upon the floor with a positiveness which fairly shook the log dwelling, and there burst out of his mouth a word of command of such explosive energy that neither dogs nor men could have heard it without fear. The hounds dropped the goose and themselves on to the floor as if they had been shot, and at a word of command crawled grovelling in shame to the old man's feet.

"Pups," said the Trapper in a stern voice, that gradually gentled as he continued, "I be heartily ashamed of ye! Ye have acted like men, and not like dogs of good breedin'. Ye grew stingy in yer abundance, Sport; and, Rover, ye envied the good-fortin' of yer mate, and hated him because of his good-luck. Yis, ye acted like men who fight over the gifts of the Lord, and make the bestowments of his marcy help on their wicked feelin's. I've seed many of my kind in the settlements that acted like ye, Sport, when the Lord had gin them a bigger goose than they could eat, — fur the settlements be full of sech stinginess, — and I have seed, Rover, many a hunter in the woods envy a companion the thickest furred skin in the pack, when his own pack was bulgin' with good uns. But I never thought that dogs, as well bred as ye be, would have acted so much like men, when yer mouths was full and yer wants met, on a day set apart to remember with gladness the gifts of yer Maker."

By this time, — for the feast had been eaten leisurely, and many interruptions between the courses, incidental to the scant service in attendance upon the table, — the evening was well advanced, and, before the dishes were cleared away and the room restored to its usual appearance, it was well-nigh the usual bed-time of the Trapper. He had replenished the fire with huge hard-wood logs, and now, in a large and easy chair, made from the crooked and gnarled woods of trees, — a gift on a previous Thanksgiving Day from the Lad, — he was sitting in peaceful and contented after-dinner mood. The day had come and gone, and in its activities and its pleasures he had been happy. If, as it has been said, half the happiness of life consists in one's ability to be deluded, the Trapper's happiness and even his merriment, were easily accounted for, for though he was alone, and though no father or mother, wife or children, — no, nor any friend, — had come in bodily presence to his door, yet in a way to satisfy the craving of his heart there had come to him, in spirit at least, the two whom above all other beings he loved; — and perhaps, after all, the friends that come to us invisibly when our mood is fine enough to see and feel their presence with other eyes and senses than our bodily ones, are at least as actually with us as those who address through sight and touch the bodily senses.

To the Trapper it was evident that this was true: that the day had brought to him no disappointment, and that to him, in the most positive manner, his party had been a success. For his face, as revealed in the softened glow of the firelight, was tranquilly happy, and the expression which softened the lines of its curves and mellowed the depth of its recesses was only such as we see in the faces of the aged when, in the happiness of a contented mood, their spirits reflect from their faces the peace into which they are passing, and in which, when they have passed into it, they will never be disturbed.

He soon made preparations to retire. He took the silver horn and the violin from the table where they had continued to lie, and returned each to its covering and to the chest. He caressed each hound, as was his custom, which they acknowledged by tenderly lapping his hand, — a mute exchange of sentiment between the representatives of two classes of His creatures which the Maker has placed in closest companionship. He then retired. His bed stood in the corner against the wall, in which was cut a window space which commanded the lake outside, and over the window the two picture frames were hung, one filled and the other empty. The Trapper, with his head resting on the pillow, gazed alternately at the frames above the window, and then at the great white world outside, above which curved the blue dome of another world, whose brightness shone through in many a starry stream.

And so the Trapper lay gazing at the white peacefulness without, and the two picture frames within, till sleep, gentle as his mood, stole on him. His senses yielded willingly to the persuasive pressure. He was ready for slumber, and his will made no resistance. He simply raised his eyes to the two pictures above the window, and, as his glance fell, his gaze lingered for a moment on the pure beauty of the world outside, and he said, "I trust the boys be happy;" and then he slept.

HENRY HERBERT'S THANKSGIVING.

"I WISH to heaven John Norton and the Lad were here!"

Those were the words that were said.

A large room, long, wide, and lofty as to its ceiling. A room builded by wealth. A room furnished with taste and yet extravagantly; in which the semi-barbaric and the effeminate stood in strange conjunction. From the horns of an elk that stretched widely above the doorway, hung vases of flowers and delicate vines that trailed their green sprangles over the savage prongs. A bison's head with its shaggy frontal, bead-like, glistening eyes, stout horns, and the red froth dropping from his half-open mouth was framed against the wall above the mantel. A pair of lavender gloves had been tossed upward and lay in the shaggy hair that curled above the roots of the horns. The floor was of oak, polished and waxed. Here and there costly rugs, with brave scenery woven in:

Hounds in full career on one; two knights in full tilt, with splintered lances — one reeling from the saddle, on another. An Indian, feathered like a chief, cautiously picking up a trail, blazoned on a third. Brackets for guns everywhere. Foils, swords, boxing gloves, pistols; some ancient weapons, curiously wrought, lying on shelves and hanging from hooks of polished steel, ivory-tipped, driven into the wall. Beneath the bison's head above the mantel, on a set of red deer's antlers, lay a double rifle, and by it a paddle, with a huge glengorm stone set into the handle knob. A table covered with food and fruit and flowers — a table with four plates, and a man at the head of the table. He had been eating. Perhaps he had finished the meal. Perhaps he had stopped in the midst of it. Be that as it may, the man lifted his eyes to the double rifle resting on the deer's antlers, and at the paddle in which the stone was blazing; gazed at them as one gazes when his eyes are full of memories. And then, as he lowered his eyes to the table, and his head drooped slightly forward, said:

"I wish to heaven John Norton and the Lad were here!"

A noise outside the door; a noise in the great hall beyond; a noise of feet that brushed along and fell lightly; a noise of dogs rushing forward and held stoutly back; a noise of servants' voices expostulating, ejaculating, directing. A noise that moved, came on, — and as the great door swung open, burst with clatter and tumult into the room.

"*John Norton!*"

It was a shout; — a shout that burst into the air as a bomb explodes; a shout that bore the heart out of the mouth with it; a shout that plucked the body up from out the chair, planted it on its feet, and sent it with a mighty leap toward the open door, the struggling hounds, and the great broad-chested man that stood braced, holding them back; a shout that man gives but seldom, and never save when heart and soul go out in such welcome as a friend receives when he comes unexpectedly into a comrade's presence that was longing for him.

"*John Norton!*"

"Sartin, boy, sartin," said the Trapper. "That's my name for sartin;" and his great face glowed and beamed as he shook the other's hand. "Yis, here be me and the pups; and ef ye'll look jest by the door post there, ye'll see somebody else."

As he spoke a tall, slim form stepped forward from the shadow of the door in which it had been standing, and a long, thin hand at the end of a long thin arm met the palm swept out to receive it: and so Herbert and the Trapper and the Lad met in Herbert's house on Thanksgiving night.

So these three men stood looking as they held each other's hands — looking at each other. Perhaps they said something, perhaps they didn't. If they did speak I doubt if they knew it. Strong men, steady and self-poised. Men trained as to the nerves, either of whom could die in such a fashion as to make the other two prouder of him than if he had lived. Men who loved each other beyond the love of woman. So they stood holding each other's hands looking at each other.

"Henry," said the Trapper at length, "the pups has come fur to see ye. We musn't be selfish in our greetin'. They be well-mannered, but a word from ye and a tech of yer hand will fetch the heart from atween their ribs."

That sentence broke the silence — broke the quiet and charm of it, — and in an instant Herbert was with the dogs, or rather the dogs were on Herbert: their paws on his shoulder; their tongues on his face, and his arms around their bodies hugging them. And then down the three went on to the rug, — the rug on which he had had their pictures woven in bright colors — playing with them; playing with abandon, as a hunter plays with his dogs when dogs and man are in frolicsome mood. What feints he made at them; what dashes they at him! What crouchings and leaps; and then the tumble in a heap, while the man's voice in laughter and the dogs' deep bayings rose and swelled till the air of the room vibrated to the ceiling.

"Hi, pups! hi, pups!" called the Trapper who stood himself laughing at the boisterous play. "Hi, pups, away with yer nonsense, and git ye up from the floor, boy; yer mats aint skins, and ye'll have them in threads ef ye aint keerful. Lord, how the pups will dream of this when they're back in the cabin, and the wind storms over the chimney, and they lie quiverin' in their gladness as their memories work when they be asleep on their hearthstun."

The dogs obeyed the call of their master and seated themselves on their haunches demurely in outward appearance, but with eyes still glistening. The Trapper stood and scanned the room. He looked at the pictures on the wall, the stretch of the antlers, the bison's head, the double gun and the paddle. He looked at the polished floor, the blazoned rugs, and then at the table bright with dishes such as his eyes had never beheld: looked as a man looks with eyes trained to note the minutest thing and take the parts and the whole all in at a glance, and then he turned his eyes upon the young man and said:

"And this is yer cabin, boy?"

"Yes," answered Herbert. "This is my cabin, old friend; mine and yours and the Lad's."

"It be well said, boy," answered the Trapper; "yis it be well said. It be different from mine, but the heart and the greetin' makes it the same." And he looked at Herbert with eyes that brimmed, and added, as if speaking to himself, but half turning to the lad, "it be different than ourn, but the heart and the greetin', Lad, makes it the same."

"I'm glad you have come just as you have," said Herbert, "for I was on the point of eating my Thanksgiving dinner. The table is spread, you see, and the dishes are ready."

"Ye don't mean to say, boy, that ye cooked all these things yerself?" asked the Trapper, as he looked at the dozen and one preparations under which the table fairly groaned.

"No," answered Herbert, "I didn't. In the cities we have cooks that cook for us; for we are too busy to do our own cooking."

"Hoot, boy," answered the Trapper, "ye be sartinly off the trail, there. I can't conceit that a man can be too busy to cook his own vittals; for when he cooks his own vittals, he cooks 'em for his own mouth, and it makes safe eatin'. I trust yer cook, as ye call him, boy, is a man that can be trusted."

"My cook," answered Herbert, "is a woman. We have very few men cooks in the city."

"I dunno, I dunno," said the Trapper incredulously, "it may be safe cookin' as ye say; but I never knowed a squaw, or a white woman either, that a man that was at all tasty could trust in the matter of his vittals, onless it was in the makin' of pies and cake and sech leetle things that don't stay in a man's stomach half long enough, or else stay in his stomach a good deal too long. I eat a pie up here at a shanty on the Connecticut that has stayed with me ever sence, and the longer it stays the heavier it gits, and the pressure be a good deal like the gripes. I hadn't more'n got it down afore I knowed it wasn't honest cookin', and I gin the woman that peddled it to me, a piece of my mind. The Lad said she wasn't to blame, and it may be she wasn't; but that don't make any difference with a man with a stun in his stomach. Somebody is to blame, and I took a lick at the fust one that I could fasten it on; and I told the Lad — for he argued the p'int with me like a missioner — I told the Lad that ef I hadn't got the right un the Lord would see to that. But ef ye say the cookin' is honest, Henry, I'll believe ye, for ye know what good cookin' is, especially in the matter of meats; for I edicated ye myself." So saying, the old man proceeded toward the table and prepared to seat himself.

"Not there, not there!" exclaimed Herbert, "your place is at the head of the table. Take the chair at the head of the table, old friend. The house and the table and all you see, are yours. You are the father and we are the boys."

"The cabin sartinly looks as ef it was well built," answered the Trapper, as he looked at the solid oak walls, "and I don't doubt it will stand a good blow. The table is a big un and the vittals plenty. It may be that the cookin' is honest; ef ye say it is, it is, but I sartinly have doubts of the woman. But as to my takin' the head of the table, boy, that be another thing, and I conceit it isn't right, for the man that owns the cabin owns the table in it, and them that come to the table be his guests, and the place of honor be his, for he sarves them, and it be sarvin' that makes honor. Yis, boy, it be sarvin' that makes honor. And there be another p'int: ye've called me father, and ye say that the Lad and ye be boys; and the white in my head and the feelin' of my sperit towards ye make it fit that the word should be as ye said it, for all the young be boys and girls to the old; and the old be fathers and mothers to all the young ef their sperit be right. But a father loves to see his boy in the place of honor, and I've come on a long trail, boy, to see ye in yer own cabin and at yer own table; and I'd rather sit furder down and see ye at the head of the table, Henry; for then I shall see what I've come fur to see — see ye in yer own cabin, at yer own table, and in the seat of honor. For there is no place so honorable," said the old man, speaking with true majesty of utterance, "there is no place so honorable for a man to be seated, as in his own cabin, at the head of his own table, with his family and friends ranged round him, on Thanksgivin' Day, when with feastin' and merriment he keeps the good old custom up."

"Henry," said the Trapper, as they all seated themselves at the table, "I ax yer pardin ef I be sayin' anything agin manners, but there be one plate too many or else there be one eater too few. The cabins be thick hereabouts, and down in the swale to the north-east, as the Lad and me come up along the line of the blazin', I seed a good many standin' round that looked to me as ef they'd been standin' round a good while; and I told the Lad that I didn't understand why they looked so gant, and why they wasn't in their cabins overseein' the cookin."

"I doubt if some of them you saw, John Norton, had any houses at all, or" —

"No housen, boy," interrupted the Trapper; "why, the housens be thicker down in the swale there than fur on a beaver's pelt; and they have actually growed out over the trail, some of 'em, as ef they would shet the very sky from the sight of the trail underneath. Ye don't mean to tell me, boy, that there be any people in this settlement without housen, do ye?"

"There are certainly many, John Norton, not only without houses, but who haven't a place to lay their head, unless it be in the open street."

"God of marcy, Henry!" exclaimed the Trapper, "do ye mean to say that there is a man in this settlement to-day that hasn't a Thanksgivin' table to go to, or that there is a man that has no better place to sleep than the stuns of the paved carries? Why, boy, they be colder than a coffin."

"I am sorry to say, John Norton," answered the young man, "that the facts are as I have stated."

"Henry," replied the Trapper, as he rose from his chair, "there be a man standin' down in the swale over here beside an elm with a cracked trunk and an iron band round it; leastwise, he was standin' there when me and the Lad come by, — that looked as ef he had been lost in the woods for a month, and had lived on the memory of vittals he had eat when a boy, for his face was pinched and the place where ye tighten the belt looked holler. Ef ye've no objection I'll go down and fetch him up and set him by the plate there. The vittals will taste sweeter in our mouths ef the sweetness, as we eat, be in his'n. I see ye have a plenty, boy; and ef the meat should gin out and the woman be onsartin, I've got some jerked venison in my pack that I brought as a sort of a gift to ye, that'll stay by the man, ef he be reasonably good at swallerin', ontil he gets luck in his huntin'. Have ye got any objection, boy?"

"No, no, John Norton," replied the young man; "for God's sake, go and bring him in. It shan't be said that a man goes hungry to-day, if he can come to my house; and I'm ashamed, old friend, that I myself haven't found him — and not you."

"It is all in the eye, boy," answered the Trapper; "yis, it be all in the eye. Yer eye gits keen in the woods; but the settlements blind ye. He stood in the shadder of the tree, pinched up agin the bark; but I noted him, and his look was the look of a starvin' man. I'll have him here in a minute. He's there yit, I'll warrant; for he looked a good deal like an icicle that's froze to the bark."

"You had better let me go with you, John Norton," answered Herbert; "the streets are very narrow and crooked, and I am afraid you won't find him."

"Henry," said the Trapper, as he paused in the doorway, "Ye be forgitful. Yer trails be a good deal mixed, and the Lord only knows how they come to cross each other so often; but I took the p'ints of the compass as I ris the hill, and I'll go as straight to the man as a bee steers for his hole, — leastwise, as straight as a bee could ef he had to foller the onreasonable crookedness of yer trails here."

So saying, the Trapper disappeared. But the door opened the next instant, and the head of the Trapper re-appeared, and he said:

"Henry, ye might as well speak a word to the man that keeps the door of the cabin, for he was a leetle sassy to me and the Lad when we knocked for entrance; and I shouldn't stop to argue the p'int with him the next time. So it may be ye'd better speak to the vagabond to save any onpleasantness when I come back. I sartinly don't want any foolin' at the door of yer cabin."

Ten minutes passed — fifteen — twenty — and the Trapper came — came not alone; but with him another, and that other — well, we will describe him:

Age, thirty-five. Not a day older; at least his looks did not show it. In stature of medium height, — five feet ten, perhaps, — hair brown, eyes gray, nose straight, mouth a trifle too small, face clean shaven, though the beard was beginning to roughen it, hollow cheeks, darkish rims round the eyes, and at the corners of the mouth wrinkles that stretched downward: wrinkles that seemed about to become permanent lines. The superficial expression of that face was that of hunger. Back of that, like a man lying in wait, watching to strike, watching and waiting, was a dogged look; the look of a man who has borne all he could stand and has come nigh to that point in which he will stand it no longer.

"Here be the man, Henry," said the Trapper. "I found him by the elm, as I told ye. He'll pardin an old man's sayin' so, but I found him a leetle cross, and I may say a leetle onsartin techin' my sperit. And when I told him that I'd come with an invite to a Thanksgivin' party, the man said I lied. I didn't arger the p'int with him; leastwise not as I might in some sarcumstances. But I got him out of the shadder of the elm, under a candle that stood in a box, and barnt without any wick to it, and I axed him to look at my face; and then we conversed a leetle more. I told him where I'd come from and what my name was; and I told him I conceited that he'd been on a poor line and his trappin' hadn't paid; and he said the trap he'd been on hadn't paid, and was a leetle luny-like, as I conceited, in his head. But I told him it didn't matter, ef his stomach was right; and arter a leetle more talk he agreed to come along with me. He fetched the carry a leetle weakly; but here he is at last, and ef I'm any jedge of looks, he'll help us out in the eatin' a good deal, even ef the cook be a woman. And now, friend," said he, looking at the man, "what be yer name, and what shall we call ye?"

During the conversation of the Trapper, the man had evidently taken the measure of Herbert and the Lad; for he had looked at both searchingly, with the least bit of defiance in his eyes, buttoning his coat a little closer round the throat as he looked. Perhaps he had a vest under it, perhaps a shirt under the vest; but either point was problematical. When the button nearest the throat was fixed he had busied himself in trying to pull down the sleeves of his coat, that were at least a couple of inches too short. This he had done slyly, as if not to attract attention; and it was pitiful to see the thin fingers plucking at them. And when the Trapper asked what his name might be he looked him full in the face for an instant and said:

" James Munroe."

" James," said the old man, " I be, as I told ye, but a trapper. The boy that sets at the side of the table be my companion; and the boy that sets at the head of the table be Henry — Henry Herbert. He owns this cabin, and the Lad and me have come down from the woods to eat Thanksgivin' with him; and we got in jest in time, for we found the vittals on the table and everything ready. Ye see, there be only three of us and I noted there was four plates. Ye see, Henry has camped a good deal with me and the Lad, and he's often axed us to come down, and so we come; yis, we ambushed him, as it was, for he sartinly didn't know we was comin'. But ye see, he had three plates besides his own, and I conceit that he was thinkin' of us and sot the two plates for me and the Lad, and the other plate he sot for the stranger that should come. For the boy's heart be a good un, and he knows that them that be rich should have one plate for themselves and one plate for them that be poor. And as I looked at the plate I thought of ye, and the boy told me to go and fetch ye, and we four would eat Thanksgivin' together. Now, as I have told ye all there is to tell, and who we be, there is no reason why we shouldn't sot down and begin." And the Trapper moved towards his chair.

But the man never moved, but stood in his tracks looking first at one and then at the other, then at the table, and then at the chair in front of the plate that the Trapper had told him was set for him.

"Come, hist along," said the Trapper to him, speaking in a cheerful voice, "hist along toward yer chair. The cookin' was done by a woman, but Henry says it be honest, and the vittals be plenty; and I sartinly be empty, and ye don't look actally full yerself. Hist along friend, and we'll begin."

But the man still kept his tracks, and moved not an inch, but looked at the Trapper, at Herbert and the Lad, at the table and the plate with incredulous eyes.

"Old man, are you fooling me?"

It was all he said; but oh! with what emphasis he said it, and what a look there was in his eyes as he said it! And his fingers, how they shut into his palms and how his mouth twitched!

"Friend," said the Trapper, and he rose from the chair in which he had seated himself, "I have never lived in the settlements, and I know not what tricks men play on each other where the cabins of the rich and the shanties of the poor stand so nigh together. But I've lived in the woods where the rich and poor be alike; fur natur feeds one as highly as another, and clothes them as warmly; and in the woods we say what we mean, and we act as we feel. The boy has consorted with us and ketched our ways, and his heart be right by natur; and though I be in his cabin and not mine, and though this be his table and not mine, and though I've not cooked these vittals myself. yit" — the old man paused a moment, and lifting one hand to his head already so nearly white, he laid his palm on his gray locks and said, " friend, look at my head; then look at my face, and there be my hand. Do I look like a man that would lie? I say ye be welcome. Do I look like a man that would fool ye? I say this be yer table as truly as ourn; fur this be Thanksgivin' day, and Thanksgivin' day is for them that be poor and them that be hungry, and we be yer brothers. Sit down."

What is that strange quality in some that can make their saying simple words sound so nobly? Is it in the voice; the face; the bearing? or doth the quality of nobleness spring into life from the centre of the soul itself? Or is it that some are gifted to pour their best self out in speech, and make the words glow like a divine translation of themselves? We know not. But no one would dream, reading the plain simple words that he spoke to the ill-clad, hungry, starving man in front of him, how nobly they sounded in the speaking.

And so the feast began. The four were hungry, and they ate like hungry men. The man at the foot of the table ate as one who is starving, but whose good breeding restrained his eating from becoming ravenous. As the feasting proceeded the Trapper's tongue was loosened in speech, and the quaint humor, the sly wit, and the touches of true eloquence which characterized him, flowed out of him as a brook in spring-time flows through the meadows, now wimpling slyly underneath the trailing reeds, now breaking noisily down a little flight of rapids.

"Henry," said the Trapper, "yer woman be a good un. The partridge sartinly be a leetle dry, but the goose be cooked to a turn. Friend," said the Trapper, turning to the man, "will ye divide the rest of the goose with me?"

"No," said the man, pleasantly, "I've eaten enough. It has been years since I have had such a feast." Then he added, speaking soberly, "It may be years before I have another."

"I don't understand ye," said the Trapper,

"ye be an able-bodied man, and work brings money, and money buys feastin'."

By this time the dinner had been amply discussed, and the chair of each, by a common involuntary movement, had been slightly moved back from the table. The conversational period had come, and each was ready to listen.

"Yes," answered the man, "money buys feasting, and labor and work earn money; but what is a man to do if he can get no work, John Norton?"

"The world be full of work," answered the Trapper. "Ye don't say that ye can find no work, friend?"

"Perhaps," answered the man, "a brief sketch of my life and some of the experiences of it, may help entertain you. As I look into your faces and recall your honorable and generous treatment, I am moved to open my heart to you. The bitterness that was in it when I entered the room is gone. The world I was ready to curse, you have taught me, by your kindness, to bless. Shall I tell you my story, gentlemen?"

"Sartin, friend, sartin; leastwise, ef ye feel like tellin' it. We was strangers to ye, but them that eat together be no longer strangers. Wherever they meet they be friends. Yis, tell us yer story, and tell it as ef ye was tellin' it to friends."

The man paused a moment as if to collect his thoughts, and then said:

"I was born in this city. My family was a wealthy and honored one. I trace my ancestry to the earliest settlers. The name I have given you is not my true name. I assumed it to hide my shame. Can you guess, old man, whom you are looking at?"

"Who be I lookin' at?" queried the Trapper.

"You are looking at *a criminal*, sir," said the man.

"Did ye break the laws?" asked the Trapper.

"I did," answered the man.

"What law did ye break, friend?" again asked the Trapper.

"I stole," answered the man. "Gentlemen, you have entertained a thief," and he spoke half doggedly.

"Thieves be hungry," said the Trapper, "and Thanksgivin' Day be for the hungry."

"I thank you for your charity," responded the man, "I shall remember you old man, when some other man with less charity shuts the door in my face when I, because I am starving, go to ask bread that I may not steal."

"Tut, tut," said the Trapper, "ye might work."

"I stole, as I told you," said the man, "I stole as gentlemen steal, not like a common thief. I wrote another man's name on a bit of paper. They call it forgery in the cities. Mr. Herbert there understands it. My forgery was detected. I was arrested. I was tried and condemned. I was sentenced to prison. It was just. My heart admitted the justice of the sentence, and I swear to you that I went to my prison joyfully. I said, I will work my sentence out. I will pay the claim in full. I will come forth a man, and as a man I will start life again."

"That's right," said the Trapper; "a good many of us have started ag'in, off and on, and the Lord of marcy is never tired in givin' a man a new start, as I jedge."

"He may not be," answered the man, "but man is, and society is. Society never gives a man or a woman a new start."

"That's wrong," said the Trapper.

"It may be," answered the man; "but it is true. I have tried it, and know. I served my sentence out. I came out of prison. I changed my name that the memory of my disgrace might not stand in my way. I searched for employment: I obtained it. I served my employers faithfully. I rose in their esteem. By faithful attendance to my duty they grew to trust me. My future was bright, when one day I was called into the presence of the firm. They asked me if I had been in prison. I told them I had. They said they should be obliged to discharge me. I pleaded with them. I asked them if I had not served them well? if I had not been faithful? if I was not serviceable? They admitted all; but they said I must go."

"It wasn't right," said the Trapper.

"No," answered the man, "it wasn't right; but that made no difference, — I went. I searched for another place. The same fate met me there. I went to a third place. Two months ago I was discharged from that, — discharged not because I had not done my duty; not because I could not serve them well; — not because of any fault they found with me, but simply because I had been in prison. I could not beg. I swore to God I would not steal. I had but little money; and I made it last as long as I could; but — "

The man paused a moment, and then unbuttoning his coat at the throat, he pulled it apart, — pulled it apart with a quick, sudden motion; and then the three saw that the only garment that covered his shoulders and chest was the coat, old and thin. He said, as he rose from the chair:

"Gentlemen, look here. Is this the way for society that calls itself Christian; that calls itself just; that calls itself charitable and forgiving, to treat a man, — a man born in this city, educated in its schools, with an ancestry that goes back to the Mayflower, — because he has done one misdeed, when he has borne his sentence bravely, and as bravely set to work to rebuild his life? Is this the way to treat a man," he reiterated with rising voice, — "refusing him work when work means money and money means clothing and bread, and leave him standing on her streets, shivering in the cold and dying of starvation on Thanksgiving Day, — the day when Christian bells are ringing, and the tables in every house are loaded with food? Mr. Herbert, what do you say when society treats a man like that?"

Mr. Herbert, sitting at the head of the table jumped to his feet, stirred to quickest motion by the energy of the stranger's appeal; jumped to his feet and exclaimed! or would have exclaimed! but as he looked he could neither see *the man, nor the Trapper, nor the Lad!* They had disappeared! He looked for the dogs, but they too were gone! There was the table at which he had seated himself to eat his Thanksgiving dinner; the four plates; his own showing evidence of having been used; but the other three clean and white as when the servant had laid the cloth!

He sank back into his chair with a bewildered

look on his face. Gradually it passed away, and he returned fully to his waking senses. He lifted his eyes to the double rifle that rested on the antlers of the red deer, and at the paddle with the Glengorm stone blazing in its shaft, balanced beneath it, and said:

"Strange that a dream could be so real." And then after a moment's pause he added,

"I wish to heaven, John Norton and the Lad were here."

A STRANGE VISITOR.

I HAD been composing a section of a sermon on the resurrection, and my amanuensis had just left me — not because my ideas had given out, for ideas are not absolutely essential to a sermon, but because, owing to some unexplained cause, I had become painfully sleepy. As I have said, my amanuensis had retired; and, selecting a roomy arm-chair — an old-fashioned structure bought from an old minister's house, and in which many a dominie had probably dozed before, — I leaned the back of it against the wall, and adjusted myself for a few moments of solid comfort. I had been laboring in my discourse to show that there was nothing especially mysterious in the doctrine of the resurrection; that the natural body could be raised and made incorruptible by the same power that had originally created it; in short, I had followed the instruction of the schools. I had been invited to preach the sermon before the

Association, and when I leaned back in the good old arm-chair against the wall, I was pervaded, sleepy as I was, with the feeling of great content. The discourse was at least an orthodox one. The Association would certainly be compelled to admit that. And as some rumors had gone abroad touching my orthodoxy, I felt that I had done well to cover so strong a point.

I can't say that there was any thing very new or interesting in the sermon, but I felt that that would not militate against its success with the people to whom it would naturally be delivered; for I was then pastor of a church that didn't wish a sermon to be either new or interesting. An interesting sermon startled them. And what respectable church, fond of conservative quiet, does not abhor being startled? That the discourse was a learned one as well as orthodox, I had striven to make apparent, and flattered myself that I had succeeded, for I had read all that the orthodox scribes had written about the matter, and culled a sentence or two from each with a pleasant allusion, or a few words of wise observation properly distributed. I had, with wise foresight, shown respect for the orthodox leaders that were dead, and had put myself in a right position touching those that were living. From all these causes I felt, as I have said, in a most contented mood as I leaned my chair back against the wall, and posed myself for some original reflections.

But I was destined to be disappointed — disappointed by an interruption; for I had scarcely composed myself in my chair when I heard a sort of rustling movement near the door, and, looking in that direction, I saw that it was being slowly pushed open, and a person was in the act of entering.

"Good evening, sir," said the man, — for it was a man, — "good evening, sir. I saw your light as I was passing, and took the liberty to call upon you. I trust I don't intrude?"

"Intrude? by no means, sir. In fact I am through with my evening's work. My amanuensis has just retired. You met her on the stairs, I dare say."

"Yes," returned the man, "I saw her; but I don't think she noticed me, although I actually brushed against her garments as I ascended; but that doesn't matter;" and here he paused a moment, as if musing.

"My dear sir," I said, "while I am very happy to see you, and confess that I am in absolute leisure, and should like nothing better than an hour's chat with an entertaining person, — and I judge by the cast of your countenance that you can be entertaining, — still, I must ask you to bear in mind that you have sought this interview, not I; and, therefore, I judge you must have some errand, — some request to make, or some knotty point in theology that you would like cleared up; — if so," and here I put on my wisest possible look, — " if so, you have but to state the points, and we will do the best we can in the way of explanation of it. I have," I continued, " as you observe, an excellent library, containing nearly all the theological works from Augustine down to the present century. I should think it very queer, therefore," — and I said this with ministerial certainty, — " I should think it very queer, therefore, if there was any difficulty that we couldn't clear up."

The stranger looked at me steadily for a moment, and, in spite of the gravity of his countetenance, I thought I detected the least trace of lurking humor.

" We think very little of books where I came from," he quietly remarked; " I haven't seen a book for a thousand years."

The sentence was very quietly uttered, but it fairly took the breath away from me. But, determined that my ministerial dignity should not be disturbed by the wildest utterance, I looked at him complacently, and, for the moment ignoring the question of time, said:

" Pray, sir, what do you study where you came from?"

"Persons and things," answered the man. "Our studies are altogether concerning existences and beings. No one ever writes a book in my country: for we have no letters. Books and letters are for the blind: for infants and those whose vision is only coming. Those who have *sight*," — and the stranger emphasized the word 'sight' — "see into the heart of things and the heart of persons."

"Very remarkable," I said, "very remarkable indeed!" — I am not sure but that I threw the least bit of satire into the exclamation; — "your country would be a very poor spot for us ministers. We couldn't possibly get along without books. Why, sir, we get more than half our sermons out of books. This discourse that I am writing at the present time — and a very able discourse you will allow me to say it is, as I judge, — could never possibly have been composed without the help of a library. Indeed, I may say that it is one of those discourses that are likely to be remembered, as showing great erudition. I trust you understand me, sir?"

"Most assuredly," said my visitor; "your meaning is very plain, and I don't doubt it is a very erudite sermon. You hope it will do great good?" and the tone of his voice was interrogative.

"Well, — hem — yes, — that is, I trust the

A STRANGE VISITOR.

Association will concur in its opinions. You see, sir, it isn't exactly a revivalistic sermon: not one directly aimed at the personal conversion of the impenitent. I have been invited to deliver the annual discourse before the Association, and I have prepared this for the occasion —"

"Ah!"

It was all my visitor said; but he said it in a very remarkable tone: a tone in no sense discourteous, but at the same time peculiar. There was an inflection in it that makes it necessary in type to put one, if not more, exclamation-marks after it, in order to properly translate its suggestiveness.

"May I ask, sir, what the subject of your discourse is?" queried my visitor.

"Certainly, certainly," I replied a little promptly; for I will confess the peculiar tone of his exclamation had disturbed me a little; "I am writing on the resurrection."

"The what?" exclaimed my visitor.

"The resurrection," I repeated, — "the resurrection of the body."

I was about to say more, but a certain look in my visitor's face checked me. He waited a moment politely as if to allow me to finish the sentence, and then said:

"What body?"

Only two words, quietly spoken; only two

words put in the form of an interrogation: quietly put by a man I had never seen before; by a man who came to seek my advice, as I supposed, and yet I doubt if all the books in my library — had they been condensed in the form of an interrogation — could have brought me face to face with so great a mystery, or shamed me with the sense of so deep an ignorance, as did these two little words.

To the question I made no reply. I knew not what reply to make. My mind had long since outgrown the old faith in the physical resurrection of the dead. I had long perceived that the sin-plagued and sin-infested incasement, — the crippled, homely, sick, dissolving body in which the perfect, beautiful, healthy, and permanent spirit dwelt, — could never be regathered in its elements as the residence of the delivered soul. The old prison-house would never be rebuilt and made the home of the soul's further captivity. The captive once out of it is out of it forever. And when the freed life leaves its damp cells and gloomy corridors, and passes out of its polluted portal, it entereth into a mansion prepared for it by Him who had delivered it from the dreadful state of its mortal surroundings. And so when my visitor asked me, "What body?" I was utterly nonplussed, and knew not what to say.

"Perhaps," he said, after a moment's hesitation, "perhaps you would like to converse with me touching the matter of the resurrection of the dead. I am well informed on the matter. Indeed, I may say perfectly well informed, as I have been through it myself."

I must confess that this outrageous statement nearly upset not merely my own equilibrium, but that of my chair also. But instantly reflecting that possibly my hearing had been at fault, I recovered my balance and the possession of my feelings; so that when I asked the next question, I did it in my usual tone.

"You will pardon me," I said; "but I really think that of late I am getting a little hard of hearing. Indeed, it is quite laughable, the misconceptions I sometimes have from this cause. Now, in this case,"— and I made a gesture, intending to be both deprecating and humorous, — "I actually thought that you said that you knew all about the resurrection from experience!" and I laughed heartily, and at the same time in such a way as to constitute an apology for the misconception.

To my surprise my visitor not only failed to join in my laughter as would have been no more than polite under the circumstances, but not even the least trace of a smile could be discerned on his features. He waited quietly until my laughter had subsided, — which, indeed, was not long-lived, for no one can laugh long when he is disappointed, and a little vexed withal, at not being joined in it by his companion from whom he has expected better things, — he waited until my laughter had subsided, and then quietly resumed:

"You evidently heard me correctly, sir, when you understood me to say that I was familiar with the experience personally, for" —

"What do you mean?" I exclaimed, now thoroughly astonished, and not a little indignant that a man should enter my own room with the evident idea of imposing upon me. "What do you mean," I cried, "to make such an assertion? And who in the world are you?"

I was greatly excited, but my visitor was not excited at all. The look of his face continued calm, and the expression of his eyes perfectly tranquil. Without a movement of his features; without a shade of hesitation in his voice; without a trace of unevenness in its tone, he answered my excited interrogation as to who he was, with the astounding assertion:

"*I am a resurrected man myself!*"

There was something about the stranger's appearance as he made this incredible claim, that absolutely precluded the idea either that he was seeking to impose upon me, or was insane.

It was not merely his appearance which withheld me from any outbreak, but something more and finer than mere appearance can denote. I looked at him more closely, and saw that he was evidently a remarkable being. His clothing, which I had not noted before, was unusual; and yet I cannot for the life of me say in what the peculiarity consisted. It did not look like mere clothing. It seemed, rather, a part of himself. Its color, which had not before attracted my eye, I now observed, was but a shade removed from the tint of his complexion. Indeed, it matched perfectly with it, and with the warm neutrality of his hand as it rested upon it. If of the earth he evidently was not earthy; for to my now opened eyes he seemed altogether spiritual. Not the spirituality of a being without a body; but the spirituality of a being who so pervades his body with his own strength and fineness that it is not distinct from him.

It is astonishing how rapid the transitions of the mind are, and how completely extreme scepticism can give place to entire faith. I cannot account for it myself; but this I know: that whereas I had from my youth been extremely sceptical as to the possibility of a heavenly being visiting the earth under such conditions as to be visible — I now found myself utterly credulous that such a being was before me. Not merely before me, but was talking with me, and that unexpectedly the high privilege was mine of questioning one who had passed through the changes that divide the seen from the unseen, and which being passed through, the mortal finds himself clothed upon with immortality. I therefore addressed myself to the conversation as one who, feeling his ignorance of a particular subject, and knowing that he has every thing to learn, suddenly finds himself in the position to acquire a knowledge which shall be both entirely satisfying to himself, and of the highest moment to mankind.

"May I ask you," I observed, speaking without the least timidity, for the stranger's bearing was altogether encouraging, "may I ask you, that we may start the conversation intelligently and from a fixed point, how old you are?"

"We have no age where I live," responded my visitor. "We live in a glory not of the sun, and the divisions of day and night and years are not known. The different stages of our existence are divided by our employments, our experiences and our happiness. But we are not ignorant of the calendar of time as it is computed on this little planet; and in answer to your question, therefore, I would say that it is over a thousand years since the experience which is known on the earth as death came to me."

Now it will be confessed that my visitor had made a remarkable communication, but it had not struck me as remarkable at all. As I have said, my mood was that of entire confidence, and I don't think that any thing that my visitor could have said would have struck me as extraordinary.

"*What is dying?*"

The question actually burst from my lips. It was a question that I in common with all intelligent mortals had pondered. It was the one question that I in common with all mortals had never been able to answer. The Bible itself, luminous as it is, had thrown no light beyond a certain line. It had told of a life within the darkness, but what might be the experience of crossing the line, of entering into the life within or beyond the darkness; the time occupied in the transition; the sensations accompanying it — whether painful, whether pleasing, whether neutral, — of these it gave no revelation. How many have wondered over it. How many have questioned the problem. Some on their knees with clasped hands and streaming eyes; others with eyes that were dry because the fever of anxiety had actually parched the sources of tears. Is it wonderful, then, that with such an opportunity given — given me suddenly — the long pent curiosity, perhaps the long pent anxiety, burst through the gates of silence, and, like a torrent suddenly let loose, out of my lips broke the interrogation:

"What is dying?"

"*It is being born.*"

I never shall forget the answer.

For a minute at least not a word was said. I looked at my visitor, my visitor looked benevolently and placidly at me. The light on his countenance was the light on the face of an angel engaged in a great ministration.

"Death is being born," I at length repeated, as one who repeats a sentence musingly to himself.

"That is it precisely," responded my visitor. "When I began to pass out of my mortal body I began to pass into my immortal body. I began to die as to one structure, and began to be born as to another. The one sensation was negative, as when one falls asleep; the other sensation was positive, as when one awakes. Oh, it was delightful to awake; to feel the sense coming to you; to realize the stir of faculty and the quickening of force through the new structure; to see as you have never seen; hear as you have never heard; to feel as you had never felt, more finely, more delicately; to come little by little and so delightfully to the possession and ownership of a structure given expressly because of its perfect adaptations to the life you were; a structure that received yourself into it through every article and atom, as the old earth structure could not."

"Is that dying?" I exclaimed, interrupting him.

"It is as near as I can describe it," returned my visitor, "in your language; but your language is not an adequate one. I am not able in it to describe so fine and happy an experience."

"And the old body?" I queried.

"We know nothing of that after we leave it. It goes back to the dust whence it was called, and we know it no more, forever."

"There is no resurrection of the body then?" I said, musingly.

"None, whatever," replied my visitor. "The old body was originally good. It was capable of receiving the spirit throughout all its structure, and therefore becoming altogether spiritual; but sin entered into it, and thence it was no more spiritual, nor could it be. Sin made it mortal, — made it subject to death, — and hence a new body is given it; and from the one we pass, and into the other we enter, in the pleasant way I have described."

"It is very delightful!" I exclaimed; "very delightful indeed. I wonder God did not reveal this to us!"

"He has," responded my visitor, "at least, he has given the true suggestion; the fault is in those that read and teach, not in the writer."

"Where shall I find the suggestion?" I asked.

"In the fifteenth chapter of Paul's Epistle to the Corinthians," he replied. "You will find it quite plainly there."

"I will get the Book and we will look it over together."

"Certainly," said my visitor, "with pleasure."

Delighted with the proposition I rose with alacrity from my chair, and — awoke.

I had been sleeping.

Had I?

THE SHADOW ON THE WALL.

"CONFOUND the day," exclaimed Mr. Fenwick, as he entered his pleasant library and shut the door with a bang behind him. "Confound the day," he repeated; "nothing has gone right with me since the morning." And with this anathema against the day, which doubtless relieved his feelings, he flung himself into his favorite chair, and putting his feet against the polished fender of the grate, glared at the innocent fire with knitted brows.

In order that the reader may know who Mr. Fenwick is, whom I have thus so unceremoniously introduced to him, and the grounds he had for his vexation, I will explain.

Mr. Fenwick was a prosperous man; the world told you, whenever you asked, that he was very well off; but the world is often a great liar, as we all know, in the using of that phrase; for in the case we have in hand the gentleman concerned was very ill off, and not well off at all. So far as money goes, to be sure, he had enough of it, for he owned houses and lands and government bonds — how many no one knew save himself — but enough to yield him a liberal income, and cause the world to respect him accordingly.

Yes, Mr. Fenwick was prosperous and respected as well. To be sure, there were certain envious and gossipy folk, doubtless, who said that he was vain and purse-proud and hard-hearted, and perhaps one or two would have said tricky. They would also have told you that he had made his money by a lucky turn in affairs, which, indeed, I believe was true; that he got his first start by marrying into a wealthy family, and that, instead of growing more charitable and generous as his riches rolled up, he was getting to be meaner and meaner, less generous and more miserly day by day. Some people would perhaps have told you this, but you would have easily learned that the gentleman was a member of several benevolent boards, a director in the principal bank of the city, and that he always wrote down a liberal donation on the first Sabbath of each year toward the church fund.

Yes, Mr. Fenwick was a prosperous man, and felt that he was and ought to be respected by the community in which he lived; and ordinarily the days came and went pleasantly and peacefully, and he could stroke the vest of his plethoric self-contentment, and thank Heaven that his name was Fenwick.

But this day had evidently been set apart for his vexation and torment. Such days, like the rain, fall on the evil and on the good, on the just and on the unjust, you know, and one of them had fallen plump upon Mr. Fenwick.

He had been down to call on his lawyer in order to receive from him a report concerning the foreclosure of a mortgage note he held against one of his debtors, who was a delinquent in the matter of a quarter's interest; and was returning home from such an errand in a most complacent frame of mind, for the action had been successfully brought, and the property, worth nearly threefold the face of the note, was now legally and indisputably his; when whom should he run against but the very man who owned the property, the mortgage on which he had just pushed to foreclosure.

It is not necessary to repeat what the man said, for he stopped Mr. Fenwick in the public street, and by his emphatic expressions speedily collected a crowd around him, and what made it all the more embarrassing and vexatious to Mr. Fenwick, was the fact that it was in front of the mayor's house, who, with several other gentlemen, were on the piazza at the time. It was a most mortifying encounter truly, for indeed the man didn't mince matters at all, but called Mr. Fenwick a thief, a stealer of men's properties, a robber of women's homes, and many such epithets very rude and insulting, but the most vexatious part of this very vexatious affair was the fact that the crowd most unmistakably sided with Mr. Fenwick's opponent, and several of them, common laborers, I should judge by their dress, cried out: "That's a fact. Give it to him. He fattens on other folks' poverty. He's a regular old skinflint," and many other words to the same effect. I doubt if Mr. Fenwick was ever so mortified before in all his life, or ever had such reason to be.

But this was not all of a disagreeable nature that befell Mr. Fenwick, for, when he reached his home, he found his brother Dick, who had come up from the country — for he lived in the old place where they were both born, and found it pretty hard to make both ends meet by tilling the well-worn ancestral acres — awaiting his arrival. Now, the object of Dick's visit was to solicit help, and as the request was both perfectly natural and reasonable for why shouldn't a rich brother help a poor one?

— and yet one which he was not disposed to grant, it threw him into a great passion. The discussion, or rather his part of it, was a very hot one, and, — well, the upshot of it all was that Mr. Fenwick got into a great heat, and poor Dick didn't get the money.

Now, any one will admit that two such occurrences happening to a man in one day, were enough to upset the equanimity of any person, especially a man like Mr. Fenwick, who, while growing to love money more and more, and more and more yielding himself to the promptings of his worst nature, still had a conscience, or enough of one, to have many pricks and stings in it when he did anything it could condemn. But another vial of wrath was about to be poured upon his wicked head, for Elizabeth, his only daughter, who had given her heart to a poor but very worthy young man — Tom Carlton, by profession civil engineer — Elizabeth, we say, had given her heart to a poor lover, and would have given her hand six months before had not her father refused his permission. We suspect the two had held more than one conversation about it, and that Elizabeth, who had right on her side, and, though a dutiful and loving child, nevertheless had spunk enough for a Fenwick, which is saying a good deal, for the Fenwick temper was, and always had been, a spicy one — we suspect, we say, that Elizabeth had got tired of the old gentleman's nonsense, and put her feminine foot down in true family fashion. At any rate, the interview was a stormy one. The father raved, threatened, and, we presume, said many foolish things, as fathers are apt to do in such circumstances; but the daughter stood firm, and so they parted, the one in grief and the other in wrath; the one going to her room to pack her trunk, for you see things had come to a very serious pass, and the other had torn up to his library, where we left him, and where, with this explanation of previous occurrences with which he had met, we will join him again.

"Yes, a confounded day it has been, and I'm glad it's over at last. Thank Heaven, I have a room to which I can come, and by the turning of a key lock further intrusion out." And with this consoling reflection he locked the door and then reseated himself in his easy-chair, and, with his slippered feet upon a convenient hassock, he composed himself for a nap, and, being completely fagged by the excitement of the day, speedily fell into a deep sleep.

"'A confounded day it has been,' has it?" said a voice close to his elbow, sneeringly. "And what has made it a confounded day? Answer me that, if you can." And the voice laughed a low, mocking laugh, as if glad that the day had gone wrong with him. It is only fact to state that Mr. Fenwick was unmistakably startled at the sound of a voice so near him, for he had fallen asleep under the impression that there was no other person in the room, as, in truth, he had every reason to feel, for, pray, wasn't the room his own private room, and didn't he alone have the key of it? He wasn't only startled, but vexed at the intrusion, and, turning in his chair so as to face the door, he said haughtily: "Who are you, sir, who have intruded unbidden and unannounced upon my privacy?"

"Oh, you needn't look that savagely at the door, for I am not there at all, but right in front of you," said the voice, "and as to my intruding, that doesn't apply, for I entered when you entered, and the room is as much mine as yours."

Now, this was very strange talk for a gentleman to have addressed to him by a stranger in his own private apartment, as any one would admit; and Mr. Fenwick wheeled himself suddenly around, expecting to see the person standing in front of him, but though he looked searchingly about, no person was there, and though he saw no man or woman or child in front of him, yet he saw a strange sight, nevertheless. Yes, a marvellous sight did Mr. Fenwick see; a sight such as I dare to say no mortal ever saw before, for there, on the wall, was the shadow of a man's face, yea, the shadow of a face upon the library wall, with no person between the wall and the lamp, or in all the room, for the matter of that, to cast it there.

"You look a good deal startled at the sight of me," said the Shadow to Mr. Fenwick, "but you needn't be at all, for you and I are old friends, and for the last year I've been with you nearly all the time, and as to this room, it's as familiar to me as it is to you, for we've spent a great many hours planning and scheming together in it."

While the Shadow had been speaking, Mr. Fenwick had kept his eyes fixed steadily upon it, as if he would make out who it was whose shadow was thus before him making itself so familiar with his private room and himself, too; but owing to the fact that he was looking directly at the Shadow and the Shadow was looking as directly at him, the features were so hidden that he could make nothing at all out of them. Still there was something about the Shadow that seemed strangely familiar.

"Upon my soul, Mr. Shadow," said Mr. Fenwick, "I cannot make you out or even guess to whom you belong, and yet there's a certain something about you which seems familiar to me."

"Ha, ha, ha," laughed the Shadow, and his laugh was so coarse and harsh as to jar on one painfully. "Ha, ha, ha, that's a good one; one of your best, Mr. Fenwick. Don't know me, eh? Well! well! well!" And the Shadow laughed again — laughed? Roared, I should say, fairly roared, as if Mr. Fenwick's failure to recognize him was a most capital joke.

"I don't doubt," spoke up Mr. Fenwick, sharply, "I don't doubt that my failure to recognize you affords you a deal of amusement, but allow me to say that it would be better taste, far better, if you should not show it quite so plainly. And I feel called upon to tell you frankly that I don't like it," and he glared at the Shadow as if he would look him out of countenance. Having thus unmistakably manifested his dislike at his behavior, Mr. Fenwick proceeded to add, and he said it with freezing politeness, "You will allow me to ask why you are here, and how long you intend to stay?"

"Oh, I am to meet a few poor devils with whom I've made appointments," responded the Shadow, "and as you and I have the same ideas of business, I would like you to hear what I mean to say to them. But how long I shall stay is another question, and I cannot answer it, for I belong to another, and in him I live and move and have my being," and the Shadow uttered the sentence as steadily as if with wretched irreverence he had not parodied the scripture.

"I don't care how many you have call upon you," repeated Mr. Fenwick surlily, for he was vastly put out at the brazened familiarity of his strange visitor. "But be so kind as to remember that I've had vexations enough for one day, and am not in a mood to be trifled with by any more callers, whether they be yours or mine."

"That's the way I love to hear you talk," repeated the Shadow; "what right have they to disturb a gentleman like you with their sniffling and their begging? I know how you treat such chaps, and you see if they get a red cent out of me by their whining and crying," and the Shadow's dark face grew darker yet on the wall as he spoke.

"Thou art a coarse brute," said Mr. Fenwick to himself as he moved slightly in his chair, and with this very frank expression touching the nature of his strange visitor, he fell into a sounder sleep than before.

Suddenly there came a rap upon the door, and the Shadow on the wall said sharply, "Come in!" and a gentleman of good address, but with a very worried and distressed face, entered. For a moment the Shadow stared rudely at him, and then said abruptly: "May I know who you are and what you want?"

"I beg pardon if my call is untimely, Mr. Shadow," replied the gentleman in a deprecating tone and an apologetic manner, "but I came to speak to you about the note you hold against me, which, you will remember, is secured by a mortgage on my house, furniture, and grounds."

"Ah, indeed," replied the Shadow in a most freezing fashion. "Ah, indeed! And it's very well you have come, for the last quarter's interest has been due these three weeks, and I instructed my lawyer last week to bring an action of foreclosure against the property."

"My God, Mr. Shadow," exclaimed the man in a voice that trembled with fear and distress both, "you surely would not do such a deed as that! Why, sir, the house alone is worth nearly twice the amount of the note, and the " —

"I am fully aware of the value of the property," retorted the Shadow coolly; "I keep an eye on my securities. Yes, sir, a sharp eye on them, and I invariably follow one rule in dealing with the debtor class, — when interest is not promptly paid, I foreclose." And the Shadow straightened itself up and, with hands clasped behind its back, looked coolly, even indifferently down upon the poor gentleman, who sat pale and trembling in the chair, too overcome by the suddenness of the blow to know what to do or say.

"But, Mr. Shadow," returned the other at length, "you certainly don't understand the case between us, or the matter of a hundred dollars or so of interest overdue for a few weeks on a note secured as amply as mine is, would not alarm you touching " —

"Who said I was alarmed, sir?" interrupted the Shadow. "Gad, sir, do you fancy I ever suffer my securities to diminish in value until I am alarmed? No, sir, I am not alarmed in the least touching the security that backs up your note. I only know that the interest was not paid at the date when due, and therefore I ordered my lawyer to foreclose."

"But, Mr. Shadow," exclaimed the poor man, pleadingly, and his looks abundantly confirmed his utterance, " I've been sick, dangerously sick, and for three months I lost my salary, and my expenses were, of course, much increased by my illness, and, to tell the plain truth, some other creditors have pressed me, and between their exactions and my misfortunes my ready money is completely gone. I could not pay you the interest this week to save my soul."

"I've heard that story before — yes, several

times before — in my dealing with men that were behind in their payments," sneered the Shadow, "and if you think that old story will have the least influence with me, you are decidedly mistaken."

"Story! sir," exclaimed the poor man. "It's no story at all; it's God's truth I'm telling you, and you grievously hurt my feelings."

"Feelings! Fiddlesticks for your feelings," interrupted the Shadow. "Business is business, and feelings have nothing to do with it. What I want of you, and all I want, is money. If you have it, well and good; if you haven't it, then I shall realize on the security and get all I can."

"Mr. Shadow, Mr. Shadow," exclaimed the other, "you do not, you cannot understand what you are saying and what you propose to do. To realize on the security as you term it, is to take my house and land and sell them under the flag at a time when real estate is fearfully depressed and under circumstances which forbid to the property all assistance of proper advertisement. Such action, however permissible under the law, would, in fact, be downright robbery. Ay, sir, robbery of a man's all."

"Upon my soul, you are very eloquent, sir," sneered the Shadow, and a most scornful smile distorted his features, "and I commend you to that profession in which your gifts of pathetic advocacy will be most appreciated. But as I don't propose to have you put a definition upon conscience for my moral guidance or discuss my method of doing business, you will excuse me if I wish you good-morning."

"Hear me, hear me, yet a moment," cried the poor, cowed, and stricken man, on whom the cold-blood decision of the other had fallen with crushing force. "Hear me yet a moment, for the love of Heaven. The house you propose to sell by forced sale above my head is my home and the home of my wife and children. Mary and I were married in it; in it, too, our darling children were all born. The furniture, you remember, is all covered by the mortgage, and if you do what you say, you will sweep property, home, and all the sweet and sacred mementoes of our domestic and family life away from us with the stroke of the auctioneer's hammer. Oh, sir, for the love of Heaven do not so wicked a deed. Countermand your orders to your lawyer. Do not push it so fast. Give me a week, and I will raise the money for you. As you hope to die in peace, do not rob us of our home!"

While the gentleman had thus been eloquently and we may say tearfully pleading, for he was sorely stricken with fear, and his soul oppressed with grief, the Shadow stood and looked steadily at him; but the hard, miserly gleam in his eye never softened a whit, and the cynical smile never left his lip. When the other paused in his pleading, he coldly said: "My rule is imperative, sir. The money tomorrow, or the red flag goes up. Business is business." And with this cruel response to the other's prayer he bowed him through the door and shut it in his face.

No sooner was the door closed than a great change came over the expression and manner of the Shadow; his eyes sparkled, he laughed a low laugh, and rubbing his hands gleefully together, he exclaimed: "A good hit. A good hit. A $5,000 loan, a $10,000 place, foreclose sharp, sell quick, bid it in, then realize at leisure, $4,000 profit sure, and the note hasn't run three years;" and saying softly to himself, "A good hit, a good hit, sell quick, bid in, $4,000 profit," etc., he seated himself at his desk, and began to look over some papers.

"May the devil take thee and all thy miserly set," exclaimed Mr. Fenwick, "who in the name of business and under protection of its heartless rules art robbing men of their properties in these hard times, and turning women and children out of their comfortable homes into the streets. May the devil take thee and all thy set, as surely he will if there be justice in heaven or Satan claims his due." And he shook his fist at the Shadow, wishing in his heart that he could smell the brimstone of the impish presence he had, in his anger, invoked, and see Old Nick seize hold of him and whisk him away on the spot.

But the Shadow was not the least bit disconcerted. On the other hand, he seemed excellently well pleased with himself and what he had done, for, turning to Mr. Fenwick, he said: "Wasn't that pretty well done? About as well as you could do it, eh?" and he winked with coarse familiarity at him.

"Am I to understand," answered Mr. Fenwick, "am I to understand that this property you propose to seize is absolutely the poor fellow's all? And that if the mortgage is pressed he and his family would be made actually homeless?"

"I don't know anything about that," answered the Shadow carelessly. "If he has put all his eggs in one basket, that's none of my affair. Every one must look out for himself in this world, and the devil take the hindmost."

"But, but," persisted Mr. Fenwick, "this is wretched business, surely. Isn't there any way in which I can see the upshot of it?"

"Come, come," responded the Shadow as if somewhat nettled at the other's persistence, "don't bother yourself with any sympathetic nonsense. Business is business in this world. If a man can't keep afloat, he must sink; that's all there is to it. Every man for himself, and a sharp eye out for No. 1. That's my motto, and yours, too, eh?" and the Shadow winked significantly at Mr. Fenwick.

"It's all very well to talk about business," retorted Mr. Fenwick, "but the man's distress seemed to be real; and if he should lose his home, and his wife and children be turned into the streets; good heavens, what a miserable business!"

"Highty, tighty," exclaimed the Shadow, "miserable business, indeed! A clean profit of four thousand, at the least, on five, beside interest at eight per cent., and all inside of three years. I call that pretty good business for prudent investors like you and me. But if you want to indulge your softness for once, we'll go down to the man's house and see for ourselves what's going on there. I'll warrant you'll see crying and hear bawling enough to last you the rest of your life."

No sooner had the Shadow ceased speaking, than Mr. Fenwick felt himself being lifted and borne rapidly through the air; and as they passed over the city toward the western suburbs, the noise of its wheels and its tramping, its shouting and its cursing, swelled rudely up to their ears.

"That's the great money mill down there," said the Shadow, grinning, as he pointed downward. "Grind! Grind! Grind! How the stones go round, day and night, year in and year out! See the human hearts flung into the grists, and what fools call honor and truth, ay, and love too, pass under the stones and come out as dust. And that's the way the money is made. Ha, ha, ha!" and he laughed long and loudly.

Never had laughter jarred so harshly on Mr. Fenwick's nerves; but before he could make reply, if indeed he contemplated making one, he found himself standing in front of a suburban residence of singular beauty. The house itself was large and sightly; the grounds ample, laid out in admirable taste and excellently kept. In sooth, the entire appearance of the place impressed one with the conviction that here was not merely a house, but a comfortable, well-ordered, and happy home.

"A beautiful place, eh?" said the Shadow. "A salable place, too. Worth twelve thousand dollars, if it's worth a dollar, in six months. For times begin to lift, and people will begin buying right hand and left, by spring. Come, let's go in. It's as good as mine already. Never mind the knocking; those inside have enough to think of without noting us, I reckon." And so they abruptly entered the house.

A family, a family plunged in deep distress. The father sat with his face buried dejectedly in his hands. A girl, his eldest child, of some eighteen summers, knelt by his side sobbing. The wife, with a child in her arms, stood over him, one hand laid gently on the man's head, strong as only a woman can be when the man grows weak; with brave, sweet words she was doing her best to comfort him. A little boy, happily too young to know the meaning of human loss and grief, was playing marbles on the floor.

"Come, John, cheer up," said the brave-hearted wife; "we started once with nothing, and we can start again."

"Mary, Mary," groaned the poor man, as he lifted his face from his hands, "you know not what you say. We were young, then, and had none but ourselves to provide for, but now we have passed the middle of our lives, and I am half-broken down; and then the children, Mary; what will become of the children?"

"Does the mortgage cover everything?" asked the woman gently.

"Everything," answered the man; "piano, furniture, books, pictures, everything."

"It's very hard," said the woman, and her pale face grew a shade paler as she spoke; "but we must make the best of it, bad as it is. We've been honest, at least, John; and the promise is ours: 'I have not seen the righteous forsaken, nor his seed begging bread.'"

The brave little woman's courage and faith, thus exhibited in the midst of their misfortune, were not in vain. The man rose to his feet, and, putting both arms around her neck, he kissed her tenderly, saying, "Thou art the best and bravest wife, Mary, a man ever had." The girl, too, ceased her sobbing, and the calmness of resignation settled over the disturbed minds of the group.

"Come, Elizabeth," — Mr. Fenwick started at the coincidence, for his own and only daughter's name was Elizabeth — "come, Elizabeth," and she spoke with an effort at cheerfulness, "play us a farewell piece on the piano. I shall miss its music almost as much as you will, when we are gone."

The girl complied with the mother's request, and, seating herself at the instrument, struck the familiar chords of "Home, Sweet Home," and played it bravely through, too, although the father began to sob in the midst of the music, and her own eyes were blind with flowing tears as she played. When the song was ended, she closed the case carefully, even tenderly, and said, "Mother, I hope the new owner may enjoy it as much as we have."

"May the curse of God rest on him!" shouted the man, swept from his resignation by a sudden gust of inrushing wrath at the injustice being done him.

"John, John," said the woman reprovingly, "remember the saying, 'Vengeance is mine, I will repay, saith the Lord.'"

"Forgive me, Mary," exclaimed the man contritely, "and may God forgive me, also, for cursing one I should forgive. But the injustice of the act! the injustice of the act!"

"I know, John, I know," responded the woman sweetly, "but wrong is never righted by wrong, and if we lose all else, let us take with us to our poverty, our faith in God and our charity toward men. We shall thus, my husband, be richer than many."

"That woman is an angel," said Mr. Fenwick to the Shadow, who was contemplating the group with a sinister expression. "That woman is an angel, and she shall not be disturbed in"—

"Sh-h!" said the Shadow coldly. "Don't make a fool of yourself. Business is business. I win, you lose, is the motto. See, they are forming a funeral procession," and he spoke as if he was uttering a joke.

"A funeral procession, indeed," said Mr. Fenwick to himself, and he hated the Shadow with all his heart, that he could speak thus lightly of such a picture of human wretchedness. "A funeral procession, indeed, for a home is being brought to its burial here to-night, and a sadder burial was never seen!"

The sorrowful and sorrowing group visited each room in succession. They looked and spoke their farewells to each familiar object. At last, having made the circuit of the rooms, they paused before a picture hanging on the wall — the picture of a woman's face, calm, sweet, and saintly. And as Mr. Fenwick gazed, first at the picture on the wall, and then at the face of the woman who stood gazing lovingly and reverently up at it, he saw the close resemblance between the two, — it was her mother's portrait. "I would like to take that with us, John," she said, "but I suppose it cannot be," and for the first time the tears came to her eyes.

"Take it, thou blessed angel," exclaimed Mr. Fenwick; but as he spoke, the room, the pictures on the wall, the family group, disappeared in darkness, and once more he was sitting in his easy-chair in his own room, looking steadily at the Shadow that still darkened on the wall.

It was plain that the Shadow was uneasy, for he kept shifting his position, and moving nervously about and muttering to himself, as if he expected an interview that was likely to be most disagreeable to him, and try his courage considerably; and, true enough, a knock in a moment sounded on the door, and in a sharp repellant tone, he cried "Come in!"

The door opened in a timid sort of a fashion, and an honest looking but very plainly dressed man entered.

"Brother," said the new-comer, speaking to the Shadow, still keeping his position near the door, as if he had hated to enter, and felt he was not wanted, — "brother, I've come down again to ask you for a little help."

"I dare say you have," replied the Shadow, "and I dare say, too, that you expect to get it."

"I hope I may," replied the man, "for I am in great need, and I don't know how I can get along, unless you can give me a little lift this fall."

"You don't, eh!" responded the Shadow sneeringly. "Well, you had best find out, then, double quick, for I've given you all the 'lifts' I ever shall, and in the future you can take care of yourself, or go to the devil, I don't care which."

"I don't know what I shall do, then," answered the man dejectedly.

"Oh, you'll get along well enough; you certainly aren't naked yet, and you don't look as if you had eaten less than usual lately, either."

"These are the only clothes I have, brother," answered the other, looking down at the coarse suit he wore, that was neatly patched here and there. "Nellie spent all last evening fixing them up, so I might look respectable, at least, on my visit to you." He paused a moment, and then added: "These are all the clothes I have, brother."

"Oh, you needn't brother me so much," said the Shadow coarsely. "You are mighty affectionate, I notice, when you come begging for money."

The man made no reply for a moment. Perhaps the rough, spear-like cruelty of the other had penetrated his honest heart with a shock able to take power of speech itself away. At last he rallied and answered the taunt with: "We had the same father, I believe!" And with something akin to noblest dignity on his face, he looked the other steadily in the eye.

"And suppose we did!" shouted the Shadow in great rage that he was so palpably hit. "Suppose we did, am I to support you all your life?"

"I don't ask you to support me at all, and you know it; I've worked hard all my life, and I work hard now, as these old hands can testify;" and he held out his horny palms toward the other. "But I've had unusually heavy bills this year; Jane's sickness, you know, was a long one, and then came the funeral expenses"— and the poor man choked in his speech,—"and besides, the crops haven't turned out very well."

"Oh, yes, I know the story by heart," retorted the other insultingly, "and you needn't reel the old ball off for my entertainment to-day. If farming doesn't pay, why don't you go to work at something else that will?"

"I never had the knack of making money, as you have, brother," was the reply. "You were born smart, and I wasn't, and so you are a rich man and I a poor one. And I thought as you have prospered this year — everybody says that you have made thousands — I thought I would ask you for the loan of a hundred dollars, and take my note till next fall. I could get along," he added, "with seventy-five, but a hundred would pay all I owe, and put me on my feet for the winter."

"And what, pray, would you do with your one hundred dollars, if you could get them?" asked the Shadow mockingly.

"There's twenty-five dollars I owe the doctor; then I had a small stone put over Jane's grave. I felt I ought to do it, for she was a good wife to me; it cost thirty-five dollars, and eighteen dollars is yet to be paid. Then in her last sickness I had to be with her a good deal, for she thought no one could tend her quite so well as myself, and so I had to hire a man to help me. Let's see. I owe him thirteen dollars. And Nell wants to go to the academy this winter, for she's got it into her head to be a teacher, and that will take twelve dollars more of it."

"Oh, go to the devil with your figuring how to spend other people's money. There's ten dollars," and he flung a bank note upon the floor. "There's ten dollars — you can take that, and the rest you had better go to work and earn; at least, you won't get it from me."

But the poor man never offered to pick up the money. He looked at it a moment, as it lay on the floor, and then said, "I didn't come to your house as a beggar, or to be treated as one. You can keep your money, brother. Nellie and I will get along some other way." And leaving the note on the floor, he opened the door, and without another word left the room.

It is only just to Mr. Fenwick to state that he had been greatly moved by the poor brother's appeal, and that under the promptings of his better nature, now thoroughly aroused, he would have given him the one hundred dollars out of his own pocket; and he said to himself, "Thou shalt have the money, poor man, if I look a month to find thee." And I don't doubt he would have done it, if it was only to spite the Shadow, toward which he now felt the utmost contempt.

"I think you should have given the poor man the money he wanted," he said to the Shadow, and he spoke very positively, as if he wished him to know what he thought of his miserly conduct. "I think you should have given the poor man the money," he repeated, "for you have thousands and thousands of it, and he is your brother, and things have been going hard with him of late, and he has sore need of it."

"Ha, ha, old hard-penny," laughed the Shadow. "Ha, ha, old hard-penny, what a hypocrite you are! God's truth, man, you look so honest that I should think you meant what you are saying, and that there is a soft spot somewhere between your ribs, and my poor devil of a brother had found it with his whining for money. But you can't fool me, old flinty, for I know, and this room where you figure up your profits knows, and everybody with whom you have dealings knows, that you are a regular old hold-'em-fast, with no more heart in you than a grindstone. Pity Dick, indeed! That's a good un!" And the Shadow laughed until the plaster on the wall rattled between the lathing. But a miserable hard heart it was out of which the laughter came, and its mocking mirthfulness was like the devil's own; it was truly.

Now, there is no doubt that Mr. Fenwick would have promptly and severely retorted upon the Shadow, for, as we have said, his better nature was in the ascendant, but for the fact that his last interview with his own brother, whose name — strange coincidence — was the same as the Shadow's, had been of a character so like the one he had just witnessed as to vividly and painfully recall it. For this reason — for he did not know but the Shadow had knowledge of the matter, and might turn the tables on him — he concluded to say no more about it. But inwardly he made a resolve, for he said, "Poor Dick! I'll surely send for thee, and thou shalt have five times the sum thou didst ask of me; ay, and that, too, without note of time or interest, either."

What a pity it is that any of us should so act that we cannot curse wrong-doing when we see it, with the old prophetic heartiness!

But Mr. Fenwick had scant time to indulge his feelings against the hateful and now hated Shadow, for his laugh had scarcely died away along the ceiling of the room, when a timid knock sounded on the door, and it was immediately opened, and a young lady entered.

"Well, daughter, what is it?" asked the Shadow, rather sharply. "Speak quick, and be off with you, for the phaeton is waiting you at the door, and I don't like to be disturbed in my business hours."

"Father," said the girl, "I have come to speak to you about my marriage."

For a moment, whether from anger or surprise, or both, I cannot say, but for a moment I am ready to affirm that the Shadow actually turned pale, and I saw his black hands on the wall clinch themselves so tightly together that the knuckles stood sharply out. And even the cords ridged into sight, while the dark outlines of his bosom on the white surface rose and sank, as it were lifted and lowered by the waves of passion within. At last it found voice and said, "I must say, young woman, you have a very business-like way of introducing subjects, and, I may add, of deciding them. If I remember rightly, it was only last week that you and I had a conversation in reference to this matter, and that I then commanded you to let it drop where it was, for I would never give my consent."

"I know that you said so," responded the girl, "and I promised to give the matter further consideration, and I have done so, and " — here the girl spoke with a steady and emphatic tone — " I have decided that it would be wrong to obey you."

" Wrong to obey me ! " shouted the Shadow. " Wrong to obey your father ? Girl, what do you mean, that you tell me this to my face ? "

" I mean," replied the girl, " that in matters of the heart each one must decide for one's self, and whatever seems to the soul — where the affections are concerned and troth is plighted — a duty must be done, and no authority save God's has a right to interfere."

I doubt, if an earthquake had jarred the foundations of the house, and sent its quivering vibrations through the wall on which the Shadow rested, and shaken every black particle in him, if he would have been more astonished than he was at the announcement on the part of the girl of her decision ; for it was nearly a minute before he could pull himself together enough to reply, and even then his voice shook with anger.

" And so," he shouted, " you propose to go and throw yourself away on that beggar of a " —

" Father," interrupted the girl, " you can abuse me, but Mr. Carlton is the man to whom I am honorably betrothed, and you shall say nothing in my presence against him. And," she added entreatingly, "father, dear father, what have you against Tom?"

"He's poor as a church mouse," answered the Shadow. "He's poor as a church mouse, and his father is nothing but a miserable stonemason."

"I know that Tom is not wealthy," responded the girl, "but he has a good profession, and is getting on well. And if his father is a hard-working man, he is industrious and honest, and everybody respects him. And Tom loves me honestly and honorably, and I know I love him with all my heart and soul and strength." And the noble girl said it with the pride of a martyr asserting her faith at the stake.

"Brave girl," said Mr. Fenwick to himself, for his heart warmed toward her, as he heard her pleading so nobly for her love. "Brave girl, God will reward thee for thy constancy, and as for this old curmudgeon of a father, let him go to the devil with his threats; thou shalt not lack thy marriage portion, for I will be father to thee myself, and dance at thy wedding," and he mentally shook his fist at the Shadow, and wished he had the power to smash his black outlines into pieces.

"And when, pray, is thy marriage to come off?" screamed the Shadow, for he was now thoroughly beside himself with passion, "when is this marriage to come off, and your noble lover to take possession of his prize?"

"We shall be married this day week, God willing," replied the girl calmly, but stoutly, "and I am going now to tell Tom my decision."

"Get out of my house, then," shouted the Shadow, transported with rage. "Get out of my house, then, and take thy father's curse for thy dowry. Not a cent of mine shall thy poverty-stricken lover ever handle. Pack your trunk and begone this night, for thou shalt stay in the stone-mason's hut, or in whatever hole your honorable lover may stow you," and he continued to curse and swear at his own child, even shaking his fist at her, as she went sobbing out of the room and down the richly carpeted stairs.

"Get out of my house thyself, thou cursed Shadow," Mr. Fenwick shouted, starting from his chair and shaking his fist at the black apparition on the wall. "Get out of my house thyself, thou cursed Shadow, that forgettest the claims of the unfortunate, the ties of brotherhood, and even the sacred bond of parentage. Get out of my house," he reiterated, in a frenzy almost equal to that of the Shadow's own; "take thy black stain from off my wall and thy black presence from this room, thou sure reflection and portrait of the devil!"

But the Shadow, with monstrous hardihood, held his place upon the wall, while Mr. Fenwick stood and shook his fist and glared at him. He held his place, but not the same position, for slowly the dark, unrecognizable face that had been fronting outward began to turn; a mocking grin tightened the thin lips and curved the corners of the mouth, and in a moment a dark profile showed clearly and sharply on the wall, a profile so true to life that none could fail to recognize it.

For a moment Mr. Fenwick stood and gazed at the familiar features, with mouth agape and eyes fairly starting from their sockets, and then he gasped, "God of heaven, who art thou, thou terrible Shadow?" And the poor man quivered and shook as with a fever fit, while the startling sweat of terror stood on his brow in drops.

"*I am thyself*," replied the Shadow solemnly. "*I am thyself*, or what thou wilt be soon, if fed by the vanity and love of money you continue to oppress the weak and " —

" Begone, begone!" screamed Mr. Fenwick in terror; "begone, thou prophet of evil; take thy black shadow from off my wall, and thy black presence from out my heart! God of infinite mercy!" he exclaimed, clasping his hands and lifting them upward, "deliver me from my worse self, whose shadow is on my wall!" and with the effort of the supplicating gesture, and the energy of his appeal to heaven's mercy, Mr. Fenwick — *awoke!*

I doubt if ever there was a happier man than Mr. Fenwick when he realized the fact that he was thoroughly awake. He laughed, he rubbed his hands together and skipped, yes, fairly skipped around the room. The old, sweet feelings of youth — gladness, generosity, love — those angels that never age, had come back to his heart, from which the devils of greed, harshness, and cruelty had just been expelled, and their presence sent thrills of happiness through his veins. The holy promise was fulfilled in him, for he had lost a life and found it, and he praised God as heartily for the losing as the finding.

Yes, the Shadow on the wall had gone from his wall never more to return, for his worse self, of which it was only a reflection, had gone from out his heart, never, please God, to return either. Happy? That doesn't express it. He was so happy that he could not restrain the exhibition of his happiness. It charged its electric currents through his body. And old as he was, thin as he was, stiff as he was, had he known the motions, I think, — yes, I feel certain, — he would then and there have struck into a double shuffle!

Happy Mr. Fenwick! What a change the exit of a devil and the entrance of an angel can make, not only in the feelings, but in the appearance of a man! The wrinkles between the brows smoothed out. His lips grew fuller and more open. A hint of the old boyish mirthfulness came to the corners of his mouth. The shrunken and bloodless cheeks puffed and bloomed. He felt himself thickening as he laughed, and stroked his vest with a larger gesture of good-natured fulness. Yea, he actually pinched his thighs, for they felt as if they had suddenly fattened.

"Elizabeth, Elizabeth!" he exclaimed, rushing to the door and swinging it open — "Elizabeth, Elizabeth!" he called down the stairs. "Where are you, my child, where are you?" and, jumping astride the banisters, he slid — yes, actually slid, like a frolicsome boy — clean to the bottom, where he landed just as Elizabeth was opening the parlor door.

"My dear, dear child!" he exclaimed, seizing her, while her eyes opened wide in astonishment, and she mentally doubted his sanity. "My child," he exclaimed, as he hugged her to his heart. "Don't think your father is crazy. He has been. Yes, he has been. But he's all right now. Put on your things and jump into the phaeton, and drive round to Tom's office, and bring the dear boy here in double-quick time. And tell him he is to take tea with us and stay all night, and every night of his life, too, if the scamp don't object. As you go down, just stop at the telegraph station, and send a telegram to your Uncle Dick, at Bramblebury — yes, Bramblebury is the name. Tell him to take the six o'clock train and come down. And to bring Nellie with him, too. And tell him the carriage will be at the depot to meet him. Don't forget, now. To-night, sure. And Nellie with him; carriage at the depot. And, John, when you get back, don't put up the horses, but drive to 112 Delancy Street, and tell Mr. Harvey. No! You needn't. I'll send him a note. Yes, that's the best way. I'll send him a note; and now be off with you," he cried to Elizabeth; and, pushing her good-naturedly out of the door, he lifted her into the phaeton, tucked the robe tenderly round her, and, giving her a good, hearty smack, sent her off. But he noticed that the dear girl was all in a tremble, and as she kissed him back tears came into her eyes.

"Dear child," he said to himself, as he stood watching the receding carriage, "thou hast a good heart and true. Cursed be the day I ever spoke a harsh word to thee, love." And with this rap at himself over the shoulders of Father

Time, he ran into the house and up the stairs, taking two at a step, and seizing his pen, wrote:

JOHN HARVEY, — *Dear Sir :* I find there has been a slight mistake made in the transfer of the property against which a mortgage was recently foreclosed, which nothing but your presence will enable me to rectify. Will you, therefore, do me the honor to call at my house about seven o'clock this evening, and assist me in putting the matter right? Very respectfully, I remain, my dear sir, truly yours,
SAMUEL FENWICK.
JOHN HARVEY, *present.*

Mr. Fenwick read this epistle over twice, while his face beamed with benevolent fun. Then he rubbed his hands, and said, "That'll bring him. Accommodating fellow, that Harvey. Quick tempered, but over it in a jiffy. Sorry for the row he made to-day. No doubt of it. And his wife — the angel! When he told her of it, I can hear her say, 'John, John, you should not have done that!' But it'll be all right this evening. Yes, it'll be all right this evening." And Mr. Fenwick winked, rubbed his hands, and laughed knowingly to himself, while his feet seemed on the very point of plunging off into the double shuffle on their own account.

So the note was sealed, and placed on the silver salver on the table in the hall, where the servant could not fail to see it on his return. Then Mr. Fenwick seized his hat, overcoat, and gloves, and started down the stone steps, toward the gate, saying to himself: "Yes, yes, there's time, if I move lively. There's time. Deed made out, house opened, fires lighted, table set, capital joke, capital joke!" And thus talking to himself, rubbing his hands and laughing, the once stately Mr. Fenwick skittered along the pavement at a pace between a walk and a run, as if he was entered in the free-for-all race, while the boys playing on the street stared at him with open mouths, and the little Scotch terriers, as he rushed along muttering and laughing and rubbing his hands, scurried out of his path and whipped round the corners, where, at a goodly distance, they stood and watched him with their keen, bright eyes, as if he were a crazy man.

But little cared happy Mr. Fenwick for boys or dogs, or for men or women either, for the matter of that, for his heart was full of the blessed deed he was about to do; and was as a fountain that had long stood empty, parching and blistering in the sun, when the abundant waters come pouring into it. What deed? Ah, may you be as happy to read as I am to write it! The Harvey property was to be put back to the same state that it stood in before the foreclosure. The house was to be opened, fires kindled, lights lighted, table set, and under Mrs. Harvey's plate — no, we won't write that yet. Mr. Fenwick didn't even speak it aloud to himself, but whispered it joyfully to some listener within his own bosom. No, we won't write it yet awhile, we won't even hint what it was. Yes, it shall remain hidden from all eyes until the very last. A sweet, sweet secret, hidden safely between Mr. Fenwick and the angel that suggested it.

"Tom, my boy, I'm glad to see you," exclaimed Mr. Fenwick, as he entered the parlor of his own house an hour afterward, his hat in his hand, and his muffler still on; and he seized Elizabeth's lover by the hand and shook it heartily. "There's no use of my mincing matters, children," he continued. "I've made a regular ass of myself, and it does me good to confess it. Yes, I've acted the part of a cruel, miserly old curmudgeon, and came near doing both of you a monstrous wrong. But I've come to my right senses at last, and I praise God it isn't too late. Elizabeth says she loves you, Tom, and that you love her, and I'm glad of it, for I've looked you up a little, and find you are A1 in the record. So, you can get married as soon as you please, and God bless you both. I only ask one thing: You must live here and be my children still, and let me see your happiness, for the house is large, and it will be Elizabeth's the day you are married. And here we'll live and be happy together;" and Mr. Fenwick shook Tom again by the hand, kissed Elizabeth, and whisked into the hall to deposit his hat and overcoat on the rack, and ran, yes, actually ran, against a man and a girl standing there. It was his brother Dick and Nellie, whom the coachman had ushered in at the door, and who were thus left standing in the great hall, not knowing what to do next.

"Dick, my dear old boy," shouted Mr. Fenwick joyfully, as he threw his arms around the man's neck and hugged him. "Dick, my dear old boy, how glad I am you have come! And Nellie, welcome to your uncle's house. Elizabeth, Elizabeth," he called, "here's your Uncle Dick and cousin Nellie." And even as she was greeting them, he whispered something in her ear, and glanced at a huge bundle under the table.

"Come, Dick," he said, seizing his brother by the arm, "come, Dick, come up to the library. I've something to say to you. Give Nell the blue room," he called back to his daughter, "and tell cook to hurry up supper. Coffee and steak, and plenty of it, for Dick and I are hungry as twin bears, eh, old boy?" And he punched his big, lumbering brother in the ribs, as if the shadow that finally puts a total eclipse on our brief lives had gone back forty years on the dial, and they were only boys again. Ah, gentlemen, if the shadow on the dial would but go back, and we could start again, some of us would do differently than we have done, and win, it may be, happier fortunes.

"Dick," he said, immediately they were in the room, "Dick, I've not treated you rightly, and I beg your pardon, and I trust you will forgive me. The fact is, I had grown to love money inordinately, and was going to the devil as fast as greed, vanity, and miserly passion could send a fellow along. But I've come to myself, and all that is over, thank God. I'll be a brother to you after this, old boy. See if I ain't! There's five hundred dollars," and he stuffed five one hundred dollar bills into Dick's hand. "And I want you to fix up the dear old place, and make it look as it used to when we were boys upon it. And when that is gone, come for more. And as for Nellie, she's a sweet and sensible-looking girl. She must stay with Elizabeth awhile, and then she shall go to school as long as she wants to, and I have money enough to pay the bills;" and with these words he shoved his brother down into the easy-chair and darted out of the room, calling back from the foot of the stairs, "Dick, when you have warmed yourself, come down to the parlor and I'll show you my future son-in-law."

But poor Dick sat in the chair still looking at the money he held in his hand, while a warmth finer than that any fire ever yielded stole into his heart and quickened its beating. If tears did come to his eyes; if he wiped them away, first with the back of his rough hand, and then with an old handkerchief he fished from his pocket, embroidered with numberless holes; if he did count the bills a dozen times over, and study their beautifully engraved faces through blinding tears; and if he did, finally, get awkwardly down upon his knees, with his homely, sunburnt, massive face raised upward; if he did do all this, what business is it of ours? No, I wouldn't tell you a word about it for the five bills themselves!

The supper? Oh, yes, certainly you shall have that! Well, the supper was one of those happy affairs which occur on this earth now and then, and which memory zealously guards ever after. A favorite picture on the walls of time. No stiffness, no ceremony to occasion awkwardness, no freezing decorum, but all was cheerful, jocular, happy.

Suddenly, in the midst of the eating, the bell rang. "Excuse me," exclaimed Mr. Fenwick, "I know who it is," and jumping up, he ran to the door himself and opened it.

"Mr. Harvey, I'm glad to see you. Walk in, walk in; be with you in a moment," and ushering the gentleman into the parlor, he stepped to his overcoat, and taking a package of papers from its pocket, tied with the formal legal tape, he hurried back to his guest.

"Mr. Fenwick," began Mr. Harvey, "I wish to apologize for my conduct in the street" —

"Not a word! Not a word!" interrupted Mr. Fenwick; "not a word! I deserved it all and more too. I've done you a great wrong, sir, and I propose to right it. Here's the deed of your house and grounds, and everything is just as it was before the miserable and unjust foreclosure. And I wish you to take your wife and children there to-night; there's the keys; you will find the fires all burning, the lamps lighted, the table set and everything waiting to greet you. No, no, don't say a word, but stuff the papers into your pocket and hurry back to your family and tell them the good news." And seizing Mr. Harvey's hands in his own he shook them heartily, and saying, "God bless you, God bless you, and may you all be happy together," he pushed him out of the door, and closing it, he hurried back to his own table and began to tell stories of the fun he and Dick had, playing their pranks when they were both boys on the dear old farm together.

Ah, me, the dear old farms of the land and the dear old homesteads where we were born! Where in all our roaming have we found a spot like them? And when our heads are whiter than they are now, and we tire of the noise and rushing ways of the cities, may we all go back to the sweet, quiet, homely old places and see our suns set where we saw them rise, gentlemen!

But if Mr. Fenwick was happy inside his house, there was a happier man outside of it. Mr. Harvey no sooner found himself standing alone on the steps of the Fenwick mansion than the feeling came to him that what he had seen and heard within the last ten minutes was real and not a dream, and all that he had lost had come back to him again. Yea, that he was no longer poor and homeless, but owned a handsome property and had a home; he and his family in the world.

Ah, Mr. Harvey, many a man beside thee has had his property stripped from him by the knavery of men, and suddenly found himself homeless in a world of homes, and a wanderer through streets walled in on either side by stately residences; but few, I ween, ever in their wanderings stumbled against any such fortune as thou hast found this evening; for few of those who do us wrong see, or if they see, care for, the Shadow on the Wall,

No sooner did Mr. Harvey realize the sudden change that had come to his condition and prospects — that he not only still owned his old home, but that even at that moment it was standing all warmed, lighted, and waiting for the coming of him and his — than he darted down the steps and out of the gate, and ran along the street as fast as his legs would carry him toward the tenement house, in which the brave little wife was doing the best she could to extract happiness from two bedrooms and a kitchen, and to her everlasting honor, be it written, succeeding, too!

So Mr. Harvey ran on as fast as he could, to come to his wife and tell her the good news, and as he ran he kept feeling for the package in his pocket, to make sure he had it still, and saying to himself, "Oh, Mary! Oh, Mary!"

At last he came to the foot of the stairs, for they lived, for economic reasons, on the upper floor, and, tearing up the creaking flight, he burst into the room, and, flinging the precious package upon the table, he cried out, "Oh, Mary, the dear old home is ours again — the dear old home is ours again!" and, throwing his arms around her, he hugged her to his heart, laughing and crying in the same breath. At last he settled down enough to tell the marvellous story, and then — no, I wou't tell a word of it, how the husband ran out for a hack, and how the good wife got the wraps on the children, and herself ready to start, and how he came rushing back ahead of the hack to help her, and how all of them, laughing, crying, and talking at the same time, bundled into the carriage and were driven down through the hateful, narrow streets, to the clean, open suburbs and their own dear home.

And then the entering in. Ah! we'll see just such in heaven, friends, if, happily, we be there to see, as I pray God we may. Yes, the angel of welcome that sitteth at the gate known as the Beautiful, sees such happy entrances. But rarely are they seen here below. For even if they happen, they are strictly private, and tickets are neither sold nor given away.

But there was one "complimentary" out that night, not to a reserved seat, but standing-room only; for, as the carriage drove to the door, a man crouched like a thief lower down amid the bushes that grew by the dining-room window, and, as with clatter of feet and merry chatter of tongues, they poured through the hall into the familiar apartment, the man under the window rose to his feet and peered cautiously in, the light streaming from the lighted lamps lit up the countenance of — Mr. Fenwick!

Ah, how I envy thee, thou happy thief,

crouching under the window there in the bushes, and how I wish I might have thy luck some night, and stand under some other window and gaze upon some scene of human happiness made by me!

What rapid talking! What exclamations! What laughter! What happy tears and kissing! And as the crazy joy went on, Mr. Fenwick's face was pushed nearer and nearer to the window, and he laughed and cried, rubbed his hands, and jumped up and down in the bushes, imitating in unconscious pantomime the happy scene, as if magnetic wires connected him with those within, so that all they felt he felt, and all they did he did likewise.

But when their wraps were all removed and put away in the old familiar places; when they had made the tour of the rooms and had all — for joy sharpens the edge of that appetite which sorrow dulls — seated themselves at the table — Ah! you should have seen the face at the window then!

With nose flattened against the pane; his mouth half open in expectancy; eyes following every motion of her hands as she poured the coffee and went through those preparations inseparable from the position of a hostess, Mr. Fenwick watched for the climax, and when at last she lifted her plate and saw the note her husband owed him lying on the cloth, with the words, "Paid and cancelled" in heavily inked letters written across the face of it — one scream, one happy scream, "Oh, John!" and then, for no matter what was going on inside, then a man of precisely Mr. Fenwick's size and looks, might have been seen running across the lawn toward the road, laughing hysterically, and saying to himself: "It took her all aback, didn't it? Yes, it took her all aback. God bless her! God bless her!" and they within the house were crying at the same moment, "God bless him! God bless him!"

"And now," Mr. Fenwick said, when, some months later, he told the story of his deliverance to Tom and Elizabeth, for the two were married according to promise, and the three lived in great happiness together, "and now, as I sit of an evening in the dear old easy-chair of the library-room and gaze at the spot on which the ugly Shadow once darkly rested, I see it, thank God, no more! But a light finer than ever any lamp shed outward through its encircling shield of creamy whiteness softly illumines the once gloomy place, and I know that from it has gone, never more to return — The Shadow on the Wall."

WAS IT SUICIDE?

TWO men.

One, John Norton. You all know him, John Norton, the Trapper.

The other, — well, I don't know his name. John Norton didn't know it himself. You see the man came into his camp one day, — coming up the Racquette in a boat that was as old and broken to pieces as himself, — came into the camp one day in the morning, coming up the Racquette; and he went out of it before the next morning by the way of another river that most men dread to sail on, but which seemed to him pleasant enough — at least pleasant enough to seek it; and it is about this other river and the way the man launched out on it, and why he came to do so in the way he did, — a rather abrupt way, perhaps, some would think — that I wish to tell you.

I said I didn't know his name. That doesn't matter, perhaps. At the two extremities of life names signify little provided the circumstances are of a certain class. What does it matter what the name of a babe is if there is no one to love it or to own it? What does it matter what the name of an old broken down man is if there is no one to own him and no one to love him? Names are for the strong and those that move amid the world's activities. But the weak — the very weak I mean, and they who stand on the thin edge of the world's doing, and on the very point of quitting it forever — well, what use have these for names, and what matters it whether they have a name or not?

So we all agree that it doesn't matter what the man's name was.

What sort of a man was he? Well, there was nothing very remarkable about the man by which to distinguish him from other men. He was old, — seventy perhaps, — he was pretty well broken down as respects his bodily structure; that is, he showed signs of age. His hair was gray. It had been black once. His face was deeply wrinkled. I dare say his body had the measure of pains that seventy years bring to flesh and blood; but beyond these ordinary marks and symptoms of decay there was nothing by which to specially describe him. Take any old man of seventy years that you know, of noble countenance, and he will look very like the man that came into John Norton's camp one morning and went out of it the next.

Eyes? Well, yes, his eyes were remarkable. By the way, what strange things eyes are. What deceits they are. How they can mask themselves. How they can lie. Don't think so? Why, I saw a thief the other day on a rail car, caught in the very act, look into the face of the officer with the eyes of a saint. How frank they were! How clear and steady of gaze! No shrivelling of the lids! No variableness of the retina! No uneasiness in the look; and yet the man was a thief! But this man's eyes were peculiar in one thing: the look in them was the look of a man that never looks back, and never looks at things that are near; the look of a man who looks steadfastly for something ahead and something far away. I can't describe it any better than that; perhaps you can catch my meaning. If you don't it doesn't matter. The man's appearance doesn't affect my story much, anyway.

"Do you think it wrong for a man to commit suicide, John Norton?"

The Trapper deliberated a moment and then said: "The word is a new un to me friend. Can ye not show me the trail by some other track?"

"Is it right for a man to take his own life,

John Norton? That is what I mean," answered the other.

This time the Trapper deliberated even longer than before. He fingered the hammers of his rifle as if he were trying the lock, for a minute, and then said:

"I've seed the thing did, friend; but the sarcumstances was onusual."

"Did you say you had known a case where a man took his own life?" asked the other.

"Sartinly, sartinly," answered the Trapper, "I've seed it did. Ye see fire is hard to bear, and the redskins be cunnin' at tormentin', and to escape the barnin' I've seed men kill themselves. Yis, I've seed even officers, who ought to be rational, blow their brains out with their pistils rather than be taken alive by the varmints."

"Were you ever tempted to do it yourself?" asked the stranger.

"Never," answered the Trapper, solemnly; "the ills and the dangers of life come with the life accordin' to the Lord's orderin', and the days of our bearin' them be writ in a book, and the will of the Lord is that we live and bear up till the day comes round. Leastwise that is the way the thing looks to me. Does it not look the same to you, friend?" queried the Trapper.

"It does not," answered the man.

The Trapper looked at the man quickly and searchingly, then the look in his eyes softened, and he said:

"Friend, yer head be as white as mine, and the years that have made them white and the troubles, too, should have made ye wise. I would like to hear yer reasons for the sayin' ye have said."

"My years are as many as yours, beyond doubt," responded the man, and he looked at the head of the Trapper as one old man will look at the head of another when speaking of their years, "and my troubles have been many and dire;" and here the man paused a moment, then added, "Have you had many troubles, John Norton?"

"Nothin' wuth speakin' of," answered the Trapper. "I've felt the tech of lead several times, and the knives have got into me off and on, and I broke my rifle-stock once afore the scrimmage was half over, and wasn't really contented the rest of the fight. But these things was small matters, and sech as a reasonable man expects. No, I can't say that I've ever had any actaal trouble."

"Have you ever had any great grief, John Norton?"

"I've buried one or two that made the world

look empty arter they was gone," responded the old man.

"Children?" queried the stranger.

"Arter the sperit; yis, children arter the sperit. That makes them mine, as I conceit," and the look which the Trapper gave his companion had the force of an interrogation.

"It ought to," replied the stranger, in answer to the look. "Children after the flesh may not be children, but children of the spirit and the soul remain ours forever."

The man said this with dignity.

"I've built somethin' on that idee," responded the Trapper.

"What you've built will stand," said the other sententiously.

For perhaps a minute nothing more was said. Both men sat with grave faces looking steadily off across the lake at the mountain, which lifted its green slope up from the other side. Perhaps they were looking beyond the mountain. Most of us do occasionally. Then the man said, somewhat timidly, as if feeling his way:

"Did you ever lose a wife, John Norton?"

"I never married," responded the Trapper.

"You are strong yet," suggested the man, and he looked at the stalwart frame of the Trapper.

"I fetched a trail from Mount Seward, a good

thirty mile I reckon, yisterday," returned the Trapper.

"You must be very strong," returned his companion, and he looked at the broad proportions of the Trapper, and then he glanced at his own feeble body, adding, "I am not very strong myself. I have a good many pains. I suffer a good deal. I don't know why I should stay —" the man paused at this point. He had been talking somewhat hesitatingly — talking as a man talks who is trying to bring the conversation round to a certain point, and is not making a success of it. At last he said, as if he would get over the difficulty with one dash:

"What is dying, John Norton?"

"It's goin' out of the body, as I conceit," answered the Trapper.

"Is it any thing else?" asked the man meditatingly.

"Sartinly," replied the Trapper, "it's goin' into a body."

"The body, then," continued the man, "is a sort of house in which we live, is it not?"

"That's the way it looks to me," answered the Trapper.

"When the house gets old and unfit to live in, have we a right to open the door and go out seeking a new and a better one, John Norton?"

"The Lord who gin us the house, alone knows when it is unfit; leastwise, no hand but his should open the door, as I conceit," answered the Trapper.

"John Norton," and the man spoke earnestly, "listen. Look at this body; it is worn out. Its remaining strength only increases my pain. It is full of aches. It affects my mind. Even the gifts of the Lord are of no benefit. The beauty of the day, the glory of the night, the loveliness of the earth and the splendor of the heavens are not apprehended. My eyes are dim so that they cannot see. My hearing is dull. I only half taste my food. I tire easily. A little toil in the day fills the night with suffering. I am well, but my body is sick. The tenant is nobler and more needy than ever, for I need finer and higher things than I once did; but the house has become a hovel. Why should I stay in it?" and he put the question to the Trapper with force, almost imperious.

Perhaps it was the sudden earnestness of the man; perhaps it was the influence of the facts he had stated on his mind which caused him to remain silent; whatever was the cause, the Trapper made no reply, but remained looking steadfastly at his guest. Then again spoke the man:

"What is life? Residence in one spot? No;

it is movement. Why should we sanctify a spot and say that we must stay in it forever?—say it is wicked to leave it? Why keep the soul pent, when it would move up and move on? Are the activities of the body and the soul one and the same? Certainly not. If the activities of the body fail, why should the activities of the soul come to a halt? Why should the higher be made slave to the lower? Why should the immortal wait the pleasure of that which dies? The body was given me as a blessing. It has ceased to be such;—ceased to be such by no fault of mine; but by the working of laws inherent in its own weakness. It has not only ceased to be a blessing; it is a curse. Why should I stay in it, John Norton? Why should I not open the door to-night,—the door of my prison, remember,—and go out of my captivity into the wide liberties of the freed spirits that move in bodies that never die?"

The man was speaking, not only with earnestness, but even with passionate utterance now. His eyes glowed. His face lighted. And when he spoke of going out of the prison into the wide liberties, he swept his hand into the air with a gesture of mighty significance.

Again the Trapper remained silent, and again the man resumed:

"You said, John Norton, you have no wife.

I had one, — I mean, I have one; but she is not here. For forty years we lived together, — lived together in love. God gave us children. I was not lacking means. My fortune was abundant. Our home was all a home could be. We lived and labored together. We performed duty. We gave to the poor. But what have I now? My wife is gone; my children are gone; my home is gone; my fortune is gone; my strength is gone. I have no one to love on this side. I have nothing to do. There is no reason why I should stay. I shall open the door. I shall open it to-night. I shall go and find new strength, and new duties, and my old loves. The finding of the three will be heaven."

For a moment nothing was said. The two men sat looking steadfastly across the water at the mountain which lifted its green slope on the other side; — looking over and beyond the mountain as well. The new world lay beyond the mountain. The new world? The old, old, world, we should rather say, — the old perfect world, — old without age, and as perfect as God. The two men sat looking into it; — looking as the young never look. Why should they? Their time to look hasn't come.

At length the Trapper said:

"It may be ye be right, friend; but arter my way of thinkin' there be some things not given for mortals to fix; and the time that a man is to be born, and the time that he is to die, is not within the reach of his orderin'. I have knowed them that was born too late; and I have knowed them that was born too 'arly. And I've seed many die; and the same might be said of their dyin';—leastwise, it seems so to me. But the Lord be wise, and man be ignorant, and he alone knows when it is best for the trail to eend,—whether it be hard or easy to travel;—and therefore, I say, that, arter my way of thinkin', ye be wrong, and should wait, with the patience of a man who has seed trouble, for the Lord to gin ye release."

"I do not accept your doctrine," said the man, "for your position limits man's sovereignty. I hold that it is intended that man should have authority over his surroundings, and shape them for his happiness: where he should live is a matter of personal choice. He is to be wise — very wise — wise enough to leave a spot and conditions when they become hurtful. I am that wise, old Trapper. I am wise enough to see that my present residence forbids me to fulfil duty, to engage in honorable service, or enjoy life. I propose to leave it and seek another, where the conditions are adequate for an honorable career and an enjoyable experience."

"It has always seemed to me a leetle cowardly for a man to hasten his death," retorted the Trapper; "if the burden be heavy a man should bear it till he drops, and not shirk it."

"There is no virtue, John Norton, in merely bearing adversity as an ox bears a yoke. There must be a worthy object perceived of the mind, or burden-bearing is without significance. If there is no wise purpose to serve, there is no wisdom in bearing it. In my case the life I bear is a burden borne without an object. I get, therefore, no moral betterment; no worthy exercise of faculty; no development of the qualities that ennoble me."

Here the man paused a moment; then added: "I suspect, old Trapper, that the cowardice is not seen in our voluntary surrender of life, but in our grasping retention of it. It is the fear of death, and not reverent patience, that makes mortals hold back from the grave. Their superstition makes it a pit and not a pathway; and so they cling to life. Did they have faith in themselves; did they but know their greatness, — the indestructibility of life — the immortality of being; — that death is only an incident, weighty only because it brings emancipation from ills that be, and gives introduction to a world into which ills never come; — did they but know this, old Trapper, do you think they would race and chase the world over to escape it? Men cling to life because they fear the hereafter; because they doubt themselves;— not because they have humility enough to wait God's will. But I fear no hereafter: it is only the extension of the time that is. The God of the future is none other than the God of the present. I see him now, and I love him now. Nor do I doubt myself. I am at peace with men. I am upright in spirit. I am good enough to live. I own the future by the strength of my goodness. It is an ample bond. I have repented and believed. The Wise Man of the East spoke truth. I have accepted his truth. I have everlasting life. I *have* it, old Trapper. It is not to come to me. I *have* it now. The everlastingness is in me. I feel it. It moves like a current through my spirit. It beats like a pulse at the centre of my soul. The grave is only a spot above which, passing in my onward flight, I shall fly out of my old self and fly into a new structure and a new plumage. The old self will fall into it, and I, delivered, shall go on to infinite voyagings. This world is a thing man uses, and when he has outgrown its use he is done with it. He therefore leaves it. I have outlived its use: I shall leave it."

As the man said this, his voice lowered and a happier sound came to it as he said:

"I have outlived its use: I shall leave it. I am glad to say farewell to it and meet the sweet surprises of the future."

Again he paused. And as he looked toward the mountain, his face was bright and cheerful as one thinking of pleasant themes. After a while he asked:

"Do you know why I have come to this spot, old Trapper?"

"It's a cheerful spot for either the young or the old to visit," evasively answered the Trapper.

"I will tell you why I came here," continued the man, speaking as if he had not heard the Trapper's reply. "I came to do what I admit to be a solemn act. I came to surrender my body to the elements from amidst which it was originally called. To me it is my second birthday. I wish by a high communion to prepare myself for its happiness. I have heard of you as one wise, good, and thoughtful of strangers. As a wise man I wished to talk with you. As a good man I wished to commune with you. As one thoughtful of strangers, I wished to ask your assistance. I also wished to spend my last days on the earth amid the beauties and the peacefulness of Nature as she reveals them in these woods. In a city I should be a beggar in death. I should be compelled to beg my coffin, my hearse, my grave. Here I am rich. I own all. As one old man may claim from another old man, I can claim of you the services which friend pays to friend when spirit has departed from body. I have eaten at your table to-day. I shall leave my body to-night: you will bury it to-morrow. I would like it to have a suitable grave. Can you guide me to such a spot, old Trapper?"

The Trapper imitated his guest in rising. That he regarded his guest as perfectly sane; that he had respect for his judgment; that he accepted the conversation as utterly honest, and the stranger's view as final, — was shown by the fact that he yielded instant compliance with the strange request.

"There is a place just beyond the big rock there, that I've often conceited would make a cheerful spot for a grave; for the pines be big over it, and the water makes pleasant music on the white sand and the leetle stuns underneath. We will go and see it."

. . . .

The next morning the Trapper woke at the usual hour. He did not go to the bed occupied by his guest at once. He went and stood in the doorway. He even went to the spring and brought a pail of fresh water. He acted as if his guest were asleep, sleeping a needed sleep, and would fain not wake him; but at length he entered the house and moved with a steady and measured step to the bedside of his guest.

The man was lying on his back, his hands by his side, and his face composed with that composure, the complete tranquillity of which no earthly trouble can ever ruffle. The Trapper looked steadily at him for a moment, and then he bent toward him so as to command a view of the farther side of the body. A knife lay on the blanket, and one keen, delicately-shaped blade was open. The Trapper took it up and looked at it. The sharp point of it was colored with a stain. He stooped and looked at the wrist. It had been punctured just above the pulse; for a slight wound was there, and bloodstains were on the white skin. The Trapper reached over and felt of the blanket. In one little spot it was moist, — that was all.

The Trapper looked astonished. He gazed at the face on the pillow, white with the sure whiteness that never deceives. He looked at the knife blade with its stained point; then at the wrist with its slight incision; and then he made a re-examination of the bedding, this time closely. On it, beyond a few drops, there was no blood. The man had evidently prepared himself for the act, had opened his knife, had pressed the point of the blade into the flesh, puncturing, as he supposed, the artery; but by a misjudgment had missed the artery, and made a slight incision in the flesh that lies one side of it.

It is said that the imagination is able to kill, — that under similar circumstances men have from sheer imagination that they were bleeding to death, actually died.

Was it so in this case?

Certainly not a dozen drops of blood had left his body, yet there was the white face, and the knife, and the wounded wrist.

What killed him? How did he die? Was it a natural death? Was it suicide?

THE OLD BEGGAR'S DOG.

HE was a tramp — that is all he was — at least when I knew him. What he had been before I cannot say, as he never told me his history. Of course every tramp has a history, even as every leaf that the winds blow over the fields has its history, and my old tramp doubtless had his, and God knows it must have been sad enough judging by his looks, for he had the saddest face I ever looked at, and I've seen a good many sad faces in my day.

No, he was nothing but a tramp, old and gray-headed, and nearly worn out with his tramping. How long he had been going the rounds I cannot say, but for nearly a dozen years, once each year, he made his appearance in the city, tarried a month, perhaps, and then quietly disappeared, and we saw him no more for a twelvemonth. Inoffensive? Decidedly — as mild a mannered man as ever asked grace at a poor-house table.

Indeed, the children were his best patrons, for he had a most winning way with them, and he could scarcely be seen on the street without the accompaniment of a dozen tagging at his heels, and holding on to his hands and the skirts of his long coat. There's Dick there, six feet if he's an inch and gone twenty last month. Well, many and many a time have I seen the strapping fellow when he was a little chap sitting astride the old vagabond's neck, with his little feet crooked in under his armpits, laughing and screaming uproariously as his human horse underneath him pranced and curvetted along the pavement, and charged through the flock of childish admirers around him, as if they were a hostile soldiery and Dick was a very Henry of Navarre, whose white plume must always be found in the path to glory.

God bless the youngsters! Who of us with the burden of life's toil and care weighing us down, ever saw a frolicsome group of them, happy in their freedom from trouble and care, and did not wish he might slip his shoulders from under the load of his fifty years and be a boy again? What a pity it is that we must age and die in our wrinkles, leaving for the eye of love nothing better to gaze upon than a shrunken face, colorless of bloom and written all over with the scraggy record of our griefs, our errors, and our pains! Why cannot death charm back the boyish vigor and girlish grace to our faces, when, with the invisible and fatal gesture, he sweeps his hand swiftly across them?

The dog? Oh! certainly; but don't hurry me. I'm too old to tell a story in a straight line and at express speed. I will get to the dog all in good time, and, in order to feel as I do about the terrible thing that happened to him, you must know something about his master, for in an odd sort of way they supplemented each other. Indeed, they seemed to have entered into a kind of partnership to share each other's moods as they shared each other's fortune. And it was a strange, and I may say a very touching sight, to see two creatures, of different species, so intimately attached to each other; and often, as I have looked at the dog when he was gazing at his master, have I said to myself, "Surely, something or some one has blundered, and a human soul was put, by mistake, into that dog's body," for never — no, sir, I will not qualify it — never have I seen a greater love look from human into human eyes than I have seen gazing devotedly up into the old man's face from the eyes of that dog. How did he look? Queer enough, I assure you, for his cross, while an admirable one to yield wit and affection both, was the worst possible one for beauty, for his father was a full-blooded shepherd and his mother a Scotch terrier, without a taint in her blood.

How well I remember the dog and his peculiar looks! I remember him now as plainly as if he were lying on the rug there this very minute. He had the size of his father, and the bristly coat of his mother. His ears were like a terrier's, and naturally pricked forward. His color was a dirty gray — a miserable color; his tail had been cropped, and the remnant that remained — some four inches in length — stood stiffly up, with scarce a suggestion of a curve; he was homely, but not inferior looking, for his head was such an one as Landseer would have loved to have translated from time and death to the immortality of his canvas; with a matchless front, and roomy enough in the cranium to hold the brains of any two common dogs. But his eyes were the impressive and magnificent feature of his face — large, round, and warmly hazel in color, and so liquid clear that, looking into them, you seemed to be gazing into transparent depths, not of water, but of intelligent being. What eyes they were! I remember what a young lady said once apropos to them. She was a belle herself, and nature spoke through her speech. She came into the office here one day when the dog was performing, for he was a great trick dog, and, after watching him a moment, she exclaimed, "Ah! if a woman only had those eyes, what might she not do!" More fun could look out of that dog's head than of any other I ever saw, whether of dog or man. And though you may not credit it, yet, as true as I sit here, I have seen those eyes weep as large and as honest tears as ever fell in sorrow from human orbs. "Laugh, too?" You put that question incredulously, do you? Well, you needn't, for the dog could laugh. "With his tail?" No, any dog can do that, but he could laugh with his mouth. Why, sir, I have seen him sit bolt upright on his haunches there by that post, lean his back against it, and laugh so heartily that his mouth would open and shut like a man's when guffawing, and you could see every tooth in his head, and he did it intelligently, too, and laughed because he was tickled, and couldn't help it.

Alas! poor dog, he came to a sad end at last, and died in so wretched a way that the recollection of his death puts a dark eclipse upon the unhappy memory of his life.

Comfort to his master? You may well say that; and no man ever loved his child more fondly than the old beggar loved his dog. And well he might, for he was his companion by day, his guard by night, and the means by which he eked out the sometime scant living that the fickle charity of the world flung to him. How often have I seen the old man take him in his arms and hug him to his breast, that had, I fancy, so many bitter memories in it; and how often have I seen the dog lap with gentle and caressing tongue the tears as they rolled down the furrowed cheeks, when the fountain of grief within was stirred by the angel of recollection. But it was from the sympathy of his faithful and loving companion, and not from the moving of the bitter waters, that his aching heart found consolation.

Tell you about the man? Why, certainly; but there isn't much to tell. You see, no one knew much of him, for he seldom if ever spoke of himself. I suppose I knew him better than any one on his beat here, for I fell in love with his dog and with himself, too, for that matter, for in the first place, he was old, and whoever saw a white head and didn't love it, and whoever looked upon a wrinkled face and didn't wish to kiss it, if it was peaceful, and the old man's head was as white as snow is, and the peacefulness of a sleeping child hovered over the sadness of his face, albeit the shadow of a sorrowful past lay darkly resting upon it. But though I saw much of him as he swung around on his annual visits, and though he looked upon me as his friend — as, indeed, I was, and proved myself to be such more than once, thank God! — still he never offered to tell me his history, and I certainly never questioned him about it. For life is a secret thing, and each man holds the key to his own; and only once, if at all, may it be opened, and even then only the Father is gentle and forgiving enough to look upon the wheat and the chaff which we in our grief or our joy keep closely locked from human eyes.

No, I knew little of him; but occasionally, sitting by the fire here when a storm was heavy outside, for the coming of storms was always the prelude of these moods in him, he would begin to mutter to himself, and talk to his dog of days long gone ; of men and women he had once hated or loved, or who hated or loved him — God knows which — and of deeds he had once done, but which were now deeply buried under the years.

Perhaps he did not know that he was talking. Perhaps his soul, busy with the past, forgot the motion of the lips and ceased to keep its watch over the movements of that member which, unless ceaselessly guarded, betrays us all so often. What did he mutter about? Well, the man is dead and gone, and what little there is to tell cannot pain him now. Death makes us indifferent to disclosure, and little do we care what the world says about us when we lie sleeping in the grave, I ween. Yes, the man is dead and gone this many a year; God rest his soul, and I heartily hope he has found riches and rest and his dog ere now, as I feel certain he has, and what little I know can do no harm, if told, to any.

Well, as I was saying, when storms were brewing in the air and the sea, the uneasiness of the elements themselves seemed to take possession of his soul and agitate it, — for his very body would rock to and fro and sway in the chair when the fit was on him, and he would talk to his dog, and to men and women too, whom no one could see save himself, and if what he said might be taken as the words of a sane man, he certainly had been rich and powerful one day — and loved and hated, too, for that matter. For from his speech one could but learn that all that makes life worth the living was once his, and that he had lost it all — but whatever may have been his other losses, one there must have been in truth, for as to it his words were always the same: "*Gone, gone,*" he would say, "*gone* — and the winds I hear coming blow over her grave — but winds cannot reach her, for she lies warm and well covered, deep down in her grave." And so he would sit muttering and swaying his body in the chair, as the winds blew stormily out of the east, and the boom of the waves rolled up from the bluff, as they pounded heavily against the rocks and the shore.

Why did I not make him settle down? Because he wouldn't. I tried time and again to persuade him to it, but he never would consent. Perhaps he was right in his impulse to roam, and loved the careless freedom of it, and the solitude it gave him. For if a man would hide himself from man he must keep on the move. If he stops he becomes known. But in travel he loses his identity, and passes from place to place unknown and unnoted.

But it seemed pitiful to me that one so old and feeble should have no home, and so I persuaded him to settle down for one winter at least, and hired him a little house in a pleasant street and started him in his housekeeping experiment. But, alas! evil came of it, and I never did a deed I more profoundly regretted, for it led to the calamity I am about to tell you of, and brought upon the poor man the greatest grief that might befall him, even the death of his dog, and in a most cruel and painful fashion at that. Ah, me! could we but see the end of things from their beginning, how little of our doing would be done at times; for the benevolent blundering of our lives is as often fruitful of harm as the evil we do in our malice and passion.

It all happened in this way, and I will tell you as it was told me partly by the old man himself, and partly by those who had knowledge of the dreadful event at the time, for I was out of the city the morning the occurrence took place, or it never would have happened. I don't think any thing of the kind ever before made so much talk, or excited so much indignation.

The Legislature at its last session, not having wit or honesty enough to exercise itself over one of a dozen crying evils that were then vexing the people, got greatly excited over — *dogs!*

Some miserable curs — many affirmed they were wolves, and no dogs at all — in a remote corner of the State, had killed a few sheep, and the farmers of that region got up a great scare, and raised a hue and cry against the whole canine family. It is incredible how much noise was made over the killing of a few half-starved sheep that were browsing on those northern mountains! You would have thought, judging by the clamor, that the fundamental interests of the commonwealth were attacked, and that the stately structure of government itself was on the point of falling to the ground.

Well, when the Legislature met the excitement was at its height and the gust of popular foolishness converged all its forces at the Capitol. In due time a bill was reported, and an outrageous bill it was, too, for it not only put a heavy tax upon dogs in every section of the State, city as well as country, but provided that certain officers should be appointed to enforce the law, whose duty it should be to kill every dog not duly registered on a certain date. Even this was not all; for it stimulated the enforcement of the law by enlisting the cupidity of men and boys alike, especially of the lower and hardened classes, by providing that whoever killed an unregistered dog should be paid three dollars from the State treasury.

It was a bad law, in truth, for it was the outgrowth of senseless excitement, and an attempt to tax the affections. Property, of course, can be taxed, but we all know that a dog is not property, any more than is a boy's pet rabbit, or a child, for that matter. A dog is a member of his master's family. He has connection with his heart, not with his pocket. He is a creature to love and be loved by, and not to be bought and sold like a bit of land or a yoke of oxen, and any law aimed at the affections is an offence to the holiest impulses of the bosom, and as such should be resented.

Yes, the law was a bad one. I did what I

could to defeat it in its passage, and I broke it all I could after its passage, and that was some satisfaction to my feelings, which were in fact outraged by it; for I saw not only the injustice of it, as viewed in the light of correct principle, but that it would bear heavily upon the poor, and bring sorrow like the sorrow of death itself into families. I saw, moreover, that it was a cruel law in its relation to children, whose pretty and harmless pets and playmates could by it be violently taken from them, or actually murdered before their very eyes. Many a sad case did I hear of, the winter after the law was passed, but the saddest of all was that of my old friend, who was living peacefully and happily with his dog in the little house I had hired for him.

He was sitting one evening in the comfortable quarters I had provided for him, playing with his companion and teaching him some new tricks to practise against my return, happy as he might be, when a loud rap was delivered upon his door, and at the same instant it was pushed rudely open, and a man walked into the room and, without pausing to give or receive a greeting, he pointed to the dog, and said:

"Is that your property, sir?"

"I never think of him in that way," answered the old man, mildly. "He has been my companion — I may say my only companion — these many years, and I love him as property is not loved. No, sir, *Trusty* is not property — he is my companion and my friend."

"I didn't come here to listen to any of your crazy nonsense, but as an officer of the law, to see if you have registered your dog, and paid your tax as it commands, and if you hadn't to see that the penalty was put upon you as you deserve, you old begging loafer, you."

"I've broken no law that I know of," replied the beggar, "I love my dog, that is all. I hope it breaks no law for a man to love his dog in this city, does it, friend?"

"If you don't know what the law is, you'd better find out," answered the fellow roughly. "What right have you to own a dog, anyway? It strikes me that it is about enough for you to sponge your own living out of the community, without sponging another for a miserable whelp of a dog like that."

"Trusty eats very little," replied the old man, respectfully, "and he amuses people a great deal, especially the children; and, besides, he is a great comfort to me, and God knows that I have nothing else to comfort me in all the world — wealth, home, friends, and one dearer than all; all lost, and thou'rt all I have left, Trusty, to comfort me," and he looked affectionately at his companion, whose head was resting lovingly on his knee.

"Oh, I've heard the whining of your class before to-night," replied the fellow, "and am not to be taken in by any of your sniffling, so you needn't try that trick on me. Law is law, and I shall see it enforced, and on you, too, in spite of your shuffling, you miserable old sneak of a beggar, you."

"Friend," answered the old man with dignity, as he rose from the chair and looked the fellow calmly in the face, "better men than you or I have begged their daily bread before now, and eaten it, too, with an honest conscience and a grateful heart, and more than once when night has overtaken me, weary of journeying along inhospitable roads, and I have been compelled to make my bed on the leaves under some hedge, I've remembered that the Son of God when on the earth, to teach it the sweet lesson of charity, 'had not where to lay his head.' The lesson he came to teach, you certainly have not learned, or you would never have made my poverty and my misfortunes the butt of your scoffing."

The old man spoke with dignity, but the coarseness of the fellow's nature and the hardening influence of the business he was engaged in prevented him from feeling either shame or sympathy, for he turned toward the door with an oath, saying: "You'll hear from me in the morning, old chap, but I'll tell you this to chew on over night: that if your tax money isn't ready when I come again, I'll teach you what it is to break the laws in this city, and insult the officers whose duty it is to see them enforced against just such white-headed old dead beats as you!" and with another oath he passed out of the door and shut it with a slam.

I don't know how the old man passed the night, but little sleep, I warrant came to his old eyes, for he was as timid as a child, and easily frightened, and a threat against his own life would have disturbed him less than one against the life of his dog. But whether he slept or not, the hours of the night wheeled along their dark courses without stopping, and speedily brought the dreaded morning. I know not when he died, or where, but well I know that the memory of that dreadful morning and the woe that came to him on it haunted him to the close of his life, and embittered the last hours of it.

The morning came as all mornings, whether they bring joy or grief to us, do come. The threat the fellow had uttered against his dog the evening before had naturally disturbed him and the old man was nervous and excited, but he managed to cook his frugal breakfast and eat it with his companion. I can well imagine his thoughts and his worriment. "Law, what law?" I can hear him say, "I've broken no law. I've only loved and been loved by my dog. That's not wicked, surely. He said he'd come again, and if I didn't have the money ready. Money! what money? He knows I've no money. Tax! what tax? Do they tax a man's heart in this city? Can't a man love any thing here unless he's rich? Kill my dog! I don't believe it. There isn't a man on the earth wicked enough to kill an old man's dog, an old man's harmless dog; no he didn't, he couldn't mean that! he just said it to scare me. Yes, yes, I see now; he'd been drinking and he said it just to scare me." Thus, as I fancy, the poor old man sat muttering to himself, listening with dread to every passing step, listening and muttering to himself, while his old heart quaked in his bosom, and his soul, which had so little to cheer it, as it journeyed along its lonely path, was sorely tried and disquieted within him.

The clock in a neighboring steeple was striking the ninth hour, and the old man paused in his muttering and sat counting the strokes as the iron tongue pealed them forth; counting them in his fear as if each stroke was a knell, and so indeed to him it was, and many of the chimes we listen carelessly to, would be knells to us, if we knew what would happen twixt them and their next chiming.

The vibration of the last stroke was swelling and sinking in the air, when a heavy step sounded on the stair, and without even the ceremony of knocking, the door was pushed suddenly open, and the fellow, who had intruded upon him the evening before, entered the room. In one hand he held a rope and in the other a club.

"Well, old chap," he said, "you see I am here as I told you I would be. I've given you a whole night to study up the law."

"Law! what law?" exclaimed the old man, interrupting him, "I don't know that I have broken" —

"Come, come, old shuffler, none of your blarney if you please," broke in the fellow, "you know well enough what law I mean. I mean the dog-law."

"Dog-law! dog-law!" answered the old man, "what law is that?"

"Oh, you don't pull the wool over my eyes," sneered the other, "you know what law I mean well enough, but, to jog your memory, I'll say that the law I mean makes the owner of a dog pay a tax of three dollars, and if the tax isn't paid" —

"Three dollars!" ejaculated the poor man.

"Three dollars! when have I had so much money as that? Three dollars! you might as well have asked me to pay three thousand as three."

"Very well, very well," exclaimed the other, "the law covers just such cases as yours — covers them perfectly," and he laughed a coarse cruel laugh. "Out with the money, or I take the dog."

"Take my dog!" screamed the old man, "take Trusty; what should you take him for, you can't want him."

"Oh, yes I do, old fellow," retorted the other, "I want him very much indeed, I know just what to do with him, I'll see to that."

"Do with him?" cried the other, whose mind, perhaps because paralyzed by fear, perhaps because of the enormity of the deed, would not receive the horrible suggestion, "what would you do with Trusty?"

"Kill him, damn you!" shouted the other, "kill him as I have a hundred other curs this fall and pocket the money the law gives me for doing it. Do you understand that, you old dead beat?"

For a moment the wretched man never spoke, his lips paled to the color of ashes, and shrivelled as if suddenly parched against the teeth, and he clutched the back of a chair for support.

Twice he essayed to speak, his lips moved, but his tongue in its dryness clove to the roof of his mouth. At last he gasped forth in the hoarse whisper of mortal terror:

"Kill my dog! kill Trusty!"

It was a sorry sight, truly, and might well touch the hardest heart. But the officer of the law — God save the mark! — remained unmoved. What was one dog more or less to him? had he not already killed hundreds, as he said. The sportsman's favorite hunter, astray without his collar, the lady's pet crying pitifully in the street, unable to find its mistress' door, the children's playmate waiting in front of the school house for school to close, the poor man's help and comfort, his household's joy, guardian and friend, caught in the street on his return from his humble master to whom he had carried his homely dinner. What was one dog more or less to him, hardened by the murderous habit of his office and eager to earn his wretched fee, — what was one dog more or less to *him?*

"Come, come," he cried, as he uncoiled the rope he held in his hand, "out with the money or I take the dog."

"How much is it? how much is it?" cried the old man, fumbling in his pockets and bringing forth a few small pieces of silver and some pennies. "Here take it, take it, it's all I have — there's a ten-cent piece, isn't it? and there's two fives, and here, yes, God be praised, here's a quarter of a dollar, Trusty earned that yesterday. Let's see, twenty-five, that's the quarter, and ten is thirty-five, and two fives, that makes forty-five, and eight pennies, that makes fifty-three cents; won't that do? It's every cent I have, as God is my witness — it will do, won't it?" And the old man seized one of the hands of the fellow, and strove to put his little hoarding into it.

But the hard-hearted wretch drew his hand back with a jerk, and seizing the dog by the neck, slipped the rope over his head and saying, "the law allows me four times that for killing him," opened the door and pulled the poor dog out after him into the street.

"God of heaven!" screamed the poor old man, as he rushed bareheaded, as he was, out of the door, and hurried in pursuit of the man who was pulling the dog along and walking as fast as he could, while Trusty struggled and cried and did all he could to get rid of the rope. "Where is thy justice or thy mercy? Oh, sir; oh, sir," he shouted, running after the man, "give me back my dog, oh give him back to me, good people," he cried, for his own cries and those of the dog, too, had already drawn a crowd to the scene, "good people, tell him not to kill my dog."

It was to the honor of the crowd that they hooted the officer roundly, and called on him and shouted, "Give the old man back his dog," and greater honor yet to them that some of the boys pelted him with snowballs and junks of ice as he hurried on, and one brawny chap, sitting on the seat of his cart, struck him a stinging blow with his black whip as he scuttled past, with, "Damn you, take that, for killing *my* dog." The officer shook his club at the honest fellow and said, "I'll pay you for that, see if I don't," but he dared not stop to make the arrest, for the crowd was thickening and the air getting fuller of missiles, and every door and window was hooting him as he passed them, with the poor dog crying and moaning pitifully at his heels. Even the women, God bless them (for the feeling against the law ran high in the city), opened the doors and lifted the windows of their houses, the ladies crying, "Shame on you, shame on you;" and the cooks and chambermaids from the nadir and zenith of their household worlds, with homelier and more piquant phrase and saucier tongues, scoffed him for the miserable work he was doing, but in spite of the popular uprising, now almost swelled to the dimensions of a mob, and the verbal uproar through the hoarse murmur of which the boy's gibe, the woman's taunt and the strong man's curse, came and smote upon him in volleys, still he clutched the rope and rushed along, threatening the crowd that was closing in ahead of him with his club, and so making headway on his dreadful errand, while the poor old man, unable to keep up with him, was filling the air with his cries, and without knowing what he was saying perhaps, kept calling on the people, saying, "Oh, good people, good people, don't let him kill my dog; oh, God in heaven, don't let him kill my dog."

Indeed, his grief was piteous to see, for he was half distraught with fear, and like as a mother whose child had been snatched from her and was being hurried to death, so he, with tears, sobs and screams, kept entreating, one moment the crowd and the next beseeching heaven, saying, "Don't let him kill my dog," and being an old man and white-headed, and as his countenance and gestures were eloquent with the eloquence of true grief the people were filled with pity for him and their hearts melted with sympathy at the piteous spectacle they beheld.

Then up spake the honest carter, saying, "Friends, let's give the old man a lift, for it's a shame that one so old should lose his dog.

How much is it you lack of the tax?" he asked of the poor old gentleman as he came panting up. But he was so confused and tremulous with terror that he could not answer, and so being unable to do more he stretched his old shaken hands in which the money was still tightly clutched, up to him, but the old hands shook so that the carter could not count it, until he had taken it into his own steady palm.

"Here's fifty cents and a few odd pennies," he shouted, "and the law demands three dollars; two dollars and a half is wanted, who'll help make up the three dollars and save the old man's dog? Here's fifty cents," he added as he took a silver half-dollar from his pocket and dropped it into the hat, "it's half I earnt yesterday, and more than I'll earn to-day, perhaps, for times be dull, but the old man shall have it if Mary and I go without sugar and tea for a week."

'Twas a good speech and bravely said, and the crowd responded to it as bravely, for it fairly rained dimes and quarters and pennies, not only into the carter's hat until it sagged, but into his cart, too, until the bottom of it was speckled all over with copper and silver coin, and the honest fellow held up his hands for the crowd to give no more, crying:

"Hold, hold! Here's enough, and more than enough."

But he could scarcely make himself heard, because of the cheering and the laughing and the rattling of the pieces as the crowd continued to rain them all the faster into his cart. Ah, me, what is that sweet something in human hearts, which, in its response to human want, translates us like a flash from low to highest mood; aye, which breaketh through all barriers of selfish habit, and even the adamantine of foreign tongues and poureth out its rich largess in a common tide to meet a brother's need where'er that brother is or whatever he may be?

But the old man did not wait to gather up the offerings of the generous and sympathetic crowd, but snatching a handful of silver from the carter's hat pushed his way out of the jam, and holding the hand in which he clutched the silver, high above his head, hurried on after the officer, crying at the top of his voice: "Here's the money, here's the money; oh, good people," for the street was nearly blocked with those that swarmed thickly in the wake of the officer and he could make but slow progress through it, "tell him I have the money and am coming; don't let him go any farther; I shall never catch him; stop him, stop him, for the love of heaven stop him; here's the money." And thus crying aloud and calling, with his thin, tremulous voice, upon the officer to stop, he ran frantically along the street, as fast as he could, in pursuit.

But it is certain that the old man would not have caught up with the officer had the latter been uninterrupted in his progress, for the street was filled with people and he could not push his way with much speed because of his feebleness, but fortune, or perhaps we should say misfortune, favored him so that he shortly overtook the object of his pursuit and came up with the officer and the dog. But, alas! his old heart got little gain thereby, but a grievous loss rather, for when he came to the spot both lay stretched senseless on the ground, the man knocked flat to the earth by the fist of an indignant citizen, and the dog lying with his skull broken in by a brutal blow from the fellow's club.

When the old man came to the spot where the dog and the officer lay, he stopped, and when he saw what had happened, the money he had brought with which to deliver his dog, fell rattling, unheeded to the ground, and then he raised his palms toward heaven, as if entreating the vengeance or the benignity of the skies, and with tears streaming down his cheeks, he lifted up his voice and wept, saying: "Oh,

God, he's killed my dog, he's killed my dog!" And then he sank down all in a heap, as if he would die beside his dying dog, for the dog was not yet dead, but dying.

This his master soon perceived, and heedless of the multitude who thronged the street from side to side, he lifted the dying dog into his lap and laid his poor crushed head against his breast and mourned over him as a mother, deserted by husband and friends, might mourn for an only babe when alone in a foreign land it lay on her bosom dying; and the multitude, who, by this, had knowledge of the dreadful deed, stood in silence while he mourned.

"Trusty, Trusty," he said, "do you know me Trusty?" and his tears fell fast into the dog's bristly coat. The poor creature, now far gone in that unconsciousness which deafens the ear to the voice of love itself, still faintly heard the familiar tones, for he lifted his eyes to his master's face and nestled closer into his bosom. It was a touching sight, in truth, and those who stood close enough to see the moving spectacle, wiped their own eyes, divinely moist with the sweet mist of sympathy.

It was evident to all, and to the old man himself, that above and around and closing in upon them was the mystery which men call death — a mystery as inscrutable as it hovers over the kennel and the stable as when it enters the habitations of men, and that in a few moments the life still within the body of the poor animal, with all its powers of doing, of thinking, and of loving, would depart the structure in which it had found so pleasant an abode and so facile a medium of expression.

For a few moments nothing more was said; the old man continued to sob and the life of his companion continued to ebb away. The brutal blow that caused his death had mercifully numbed the power of feeling, so that whatever the gloomy journey he was about to take might mean to him; whether the same life he was leaving, or a larger, or none at all, he would move on through the darkness toward the one or the other at least without pain.

"You and I have fared in company for many a year," said the old man at last, " and bread, whether scant or plenty, and bed, whether hard or soft, we have shared together. Thou hast made the days brighter, and the nights shorter, by thy presence as I suffered through them, and dark will the one be, and long the other, when I see thee no more; would to God I could die with thee, my dog, my dog!"

Did the dog indeed understand what he said or did he merely sense the sorrow in the tones and seek once more, as he had done so many times before, to comfort his disconsolate master? We know not; we only know that the poor animal, with dying strength, lifted his muzzle to his master's face, and twice he lapped it with his tongue. Aye, lapped the salt tears tenderly from his master's wrinkled and pallid cheeks with his tongue; only this, for no more could he do.

"My dog," cried the old man once more, amid his tears. "My dog, the God who made thee so loving and worthy to be loved, and filled thee with such sweet feeling and the wish to comfort human woe, will not surely let thee perish. In his great universe there is, there must be, room for thee. I will not mourn thee as wholly lost. I cannot do it. For amid the false thou hast been true, and surely falsehood shall not live on and sweet truth die. Tell me, my dog, give me some sign that we shall meet in the great hereafter?"

But in response to this appeal the dog gave no motion, for, indeed, his strength, like a tide ebbing in the night, was gliding silently and swiftly outward in the gloom, gliding outward and beyond all questioning and answering, but he opened wide his glorious eyes and fixed them steadily on his master's face with such a great love in their depths that mortal might not doubt that in that love was hope and its sustaining evidence; and then the fatal dimness crept along their edges, the pure, sweet light faded away in their clear depths, and the impenetrable shadow settled forever over the lustrous orbs. The lids at last, gradually closed as in sleep, and the beggar's dog, with his head on his master's neck and his body resting on his bosom, lay dead.

WHO WAS HE?

I.

AT the head of a stretch of swiftly running water the river widened into a broad and deep pool. From the western bank a huge ledge of rock sloped downward and outward into the water. On it stood the trapper, John Norton, with a look both of expectation and anxiety on his face. For a moment he lifted his eyes and gazed long and steadily through the tree-tops and, as his eyes fell. to the level of the river, while the look of anxiety deepened on his countenance, he said,

"Yis, the wind has changed, and the fire be comin' this way, and ef it gits into the balsam thickets this side of the mountain and the wind holds where it is, a buck in full jump could hardly out run it. Yis, the smoke thickens; ef I didn't know that the boy would act with jedgment, and that he's onusually sarcumspect, I would sartinly feel worried about him. I hope he won't do any thing resky for the sake of the pups. Ef he can't git 'em, he can't; and I trust he won't risk the life of a man for a couple of dogs."

With these words the trapper relaxed into silence. But every minute added to his anxiety; for the smoke thickened in the air, and even a few cinders began to pass him, blown onward with the smoke, by the wind.

"The fire is comin' down the river," he said, "and the boy has it behind him. Lord-a-massy! hear it roar. I know the boy is comin' for I never knowed him to do a foolish thing in the woods; and it would be downright madness for him to stay in the shanty, or even go to the shanty, ef the fire had struck the balsam thicket afore he made the landin'. Lord, ef an oar-blade should break, — but it won't break. The Lord of marcy won't let an oar that the boy is handlin' break, when the fire is racin' behind him, and he's comin' back from an arrand of marcy. I never seed a man desarted in a time like " —

A report of a rifle rang out quick and sharp through the smoke.

"God be praised!" said the trapper, "it's the boy's own piece, and he let it off as he shot the rift the fourth bend above. Yis, the boy knows his danger, and he took the vantage of the rift to signal me with his piece, for oars couldn't help him in the rift, and the missin' of a single stroke wouldn't count. I trust the boy got the pups arter all," added the old trapper, his mind instantly reverting to his loved companions the moment it was relieved from anxiety touching his comrade.

It couldn't have been over five minutes after the report of a rifle had sounded before a boat swept suddenly around the bend above the rock, and shot like an arrow through the haze toward the trapper. Herbert was at the oars, and the two hounds were sitting on their haunches at the stern. The stroke the oarsman was pulling was such as a man pulls when, in answer to some emergency, he is putting forth his whole strength. But, though the stroke was an earnest one, there was no apparent hurry in it; for it was long and evenly pulled, from dip to finish, and the recovery seemed a trifle leisurely done. The face of the trapper fairly shone with delight as he saw the boat and the occupants. Indeed, his happiness was too great to be enjoyed silently, and, in accordance with his habit when greatly interested, he broke into speech,

"Look at that now!" he exclaimed, as if speaking to some one at his side, "look at that now! There's a stroke that's worth notin', and is a kind of edication in itself. Ye might almost think that there wasn't quite enough snap in it; but the boy knows that he's pullin' for his life, and the life of another man somewhere below him — not to speak of the pups; — and he knows it's good seven mile to the rapids, and he's pullin' every ounce that's in him to pull, and keep his stroke. Now, he's come five mile, ef he's come a rod, and I warrant he hasn't missed a stroke, save when in shootin' the rift he let off his piece. And he knows he's got seven mile more to pull, and he's set himself a twelve mile stroke; and there aint many men that could do it, with the roar of the fire a leetle way behind him. Yis, the boy has acted with jedgment, and is sartinly comin' along like a buck in full jump. I guess I'd better let him know where I be."

"Hillo there, boy! — Hi! Hi! pups — here I be on the p'int of the rock as fresh as a buck arter a mornin' drink. Ease away a leetle, Herbert, in yer stroke, and move the pups forad a leetle and make room for a man and a paddle, for the fire is arter ye and the time has come to jine works."

The young man did as the trapper requested. He intermitted a stroke, and the hounds, at a word, moved into the middle of the boat and crouched obediently in the bottom, but whimpering in their gladness at hearing their master's voice again. The boat was under good headway when it passed the point of the ledge on which the trapper was standing, but as it glanced by, the old man leaped with practised agility to his place in the stern, and had given a full and strong stroke to his paddle before he had fairly settled to his seat.

"Now, Herbert," he began, "ease yerself a bit, for ye have had a tough pull, and it's good seven mile to the rapids. The fire is sartinly comin' in arnest, but the river runs nigh onto straight till ye git within sight of 'em, and I think we will beat it. I didn't feel sartin that ye had got the pups, Herbert, for I could see by the signs that ye wouldn't have any time to spare. Was it a tech and go, boy?"

"The fire was in the pines west of the shanty when I entered it," answered the young man, "and the smoke was so thick that I couldn't see it from the river as I landed."

"I conceited as much," replied the trapper, "I conceited as much. Yis, I knowed 'twould be a close shave ef ye got 'em, and I feared ye would run a resk that ye oughtn't to run, in yer love for the dogs."

"I didn't propose to leave the dogs to die," responded the young man, "I think I should have heard their cries in my ears for a year had they been burned to death in the shanty where we left them."

"Ye speak with right feelin', Henry," replied the trapper. "No, a hunter has no right to desart his dog when danger be nigh; for the Creater has made 'em in their loves and their dangers, alike. Did ye save the powder and the bullits, boy?"

"I did not," responded Herbert, "the sparks were all around me and the shanty was smoking while I was feeling around for the dogs' leash. I heard the canister explode before I reached the first bend."

"'Twas a narrer rub, boy," rejoined the trapper, "yis, I can see 'twas a narrer rub ye had of it, and the holes in yer shirt show that the sparks was fallin' pritty thick and pritty hot, too, when ye come out of the shanty. How does the stroke tell on ye, boy?" continued the old man, interrogatively. "Ye be pullin' a slashin' stroke, ye see, and there's five mile more of it yit ef there's a rod."

"The stroke begins to tell on my left side," answered Herbert; "but if you were sitting where you could see what's coming down upon us as I can, you would see it wasn't any time for us to take things leisurely."

"Lord, boy," rejoined the trapper, "do ye

think I haven't any ears? The fire is at the fourth bend above us, and the pines on the ridge we passed five minutes ago ought to be blazin' by this time. Ah, me, boy, this isn't the fust time I've run a race with a fire of the devil's own kindlin', alone and in company both. And my ears have measured the roar and the cracklin' ontil I can tell to a rod, eenamost, how fur the red line be behind me."

"What do you think of our chances?" queried his companion; "shall we get over the carry in time, for I suppose we are making for the big pool, are we not?"

"Yis, we be makin' for the pool," replied the trapper, " for it's the only safe spot on the river; and as for the chances, I sartinly doubt ef we can fetch the carry in time. Ef the fire isn't there ahead of us, it would be on us afore we could git to the pool at the other eend."

"Why can't we run the rapids?" asked Herbert, promptly.

"The rapids can be run, as you and me know," responded the old man, "for we have both did it, although they be onusually swift, and there be spots where good jedgment and a quick paddle is needed."

"Why," exclaimed Herbert, "the last time we went down we never took in a drop of water."

"It's true, as ye say, boy," responded the trapper, "yis, we sartinly did as ye say, though few be the men that know the waters that would believe it."

"Why, then," exclaimed the young man, "can't we do it again?"

"The smoke, boy, the smoke," was the answer. "The smoke will be there ahead of us. And who can run a stretch of water like the one ahead yender, with his eyes blinded? No, boy, we must git there ahead of the fire, for we can't run the rapids in the smoke. Here," he added, "ye be pullin' a murderin' stroke, and it's best that I spell ye. Down with ye, pups, down with ye, and lie stiff as a frozen otter while the boy comes over ye."

With the celerity of long practice in boating, the two men changed places, and with such quickness was the change in position effected, that the on-rushing shell scarcely lessened its headway. The trapper seized the oars on the instant, and Herbert supported him with equal swiftness with the paddle, and the light craft raced along like a feather blown by the gale.

For several moments the trapper, who, by the change in his position was brought face to face with the pursuing fire, said not a word. His stroke was long and sweeping, and pulled with an energy which only perfect skill and tremendous strength can put into action. He looked at the rolling flames with a face undisturbed in its calmness and with eyes that noted knowingly every sign of its progress.

"The fire is a hot un," he said at length, "and it runs three feet to our two. We may git there ahead of it, for there isn't more than a mile furder to go; but — Lord!" exclaimed the trapper, "how it roars! and it makes its own wind as it comes on. Don't break yer paddle shaft, boy; but the shaft is a good un, and ye may put all the strength into it that ye think it will stand."

The spectacle on which the trapper was gazing was, indeed, a terrible one; and the peril of the two men was getting to be extreme. The valley, through the centre of which the river ran, was perhaps a mile in width, at which distance a range of lofty hills on either side walled it in. Down this enclosed stretch the fire was being driven by a wind which sent the blazing evidences of its approach in advance of its terririble progress. The spectacle was indescribable. The dreadful line of flame moved onward like a line of battle, when it moves at a charge against a flying enemy. The hungry flames ate up the woods as a monster might eat food when starving. Grasses, shrubs, bushes, thickets of under-growth, and the great trees which stood in groves over the level plain, on either side of the stream, disappeared at its touch as if swallowed up. The evergreens crackled and flamed fiery hot. The smoke eddied up in rushing volumes. Overhead, and far in advance of the onrolling line of fire, the air was darkened with black cinders, amid whose sombre masses fiery sparks and blazing brands shone and flashed like falling stars.

A deer suddenly sprang from the bank into the river ahead of the boat, and, frenzied with fear, swam boldly athwart its course. He was followed by another and another. Birds flew shrieking through the air. Even the river animals swam uneasily along the banks, or peered out of their holes, as if nature had communicated to them, also, the terrible alarm: while, like the roar of a cataract, — dull, heavy, portentous, — the wrath of the flames rolled ominously through the air.

Amid the sickening smoke which was already rolling in volumes over the boat, and the terrible uproar and confusion of nature, Herbert and the trapper kept steadily to their task. But every moment the line of fire gained on them. The smoke was already at intervals stifling, and the heat of the coming conflagration getting unbearable. Brands began to fall hissing into the water. Twice had Herbert flung a blazing fragment out of the boat. And so in a race literally for life, with the flames chasing them, and their lives in jeopardy, they turned the last bend above the carry which began at the head of the rapids. But it was too late: the fiery fragments blown ahead by the high wind had fallen in front of them, and the landing at the carry itself was actually enveloped in smoke and flame.

"The fire be ahead of us, boy!" exclaimed the trapper, "and death is sartinly comin' behind. The odds be agin us to start with, for the smoke is thick and the fire will be in the bends at least half the way down, but it's our only chance; we must run the rapids."

"What about the dogs?"

"The pups must shirk for themselves," answered the old man, "I'm sorry, but the rapids be swift and the waters shaller on the first half of the stretch. And the pups settle the boat half an inch, ef they settle it a hair. Yis, overboard with ye, pups! overboard with ye!" commanded the trapper. "Ye must use the gifts the Lord has gin ye now, or git singed. I advise ye to keep with the current and come down trailin' the boat; for man's reason is better than dogs' reason, techin' currents and eddies, not to speak of falls. But take yer own way; for yer lives be in jeopardy with yer master's, and ye ought, for sartin, to have the chance of dyin' as ye like to. But yer best chance is to foller the boat, as I jedge."

The trapper had continued to talk as if addressing members of the human, and not the canine, species; and long before he had finished his remarks, the hounds had taken to the water and were swimming with all their power directly in the wake of the boat, as if they had actually understood their master's injunction, and were, indeed, determined to shoot the rapids in his wake.

The conflagration was now at its fiercest heat. The smoke whirled upward in mighty eddies, or rolled along in huge convolutions. Through the fleecy rolls here and there tongues of flame shot fiercely. The river steamed. The roar of the rushing flames was deafening. The tops of the huge pines that stood along the banks would wave and toss as the fiery line reached them, and then burst into blaze, as if they were but the mighty torches that lighted the path of the passing destruction. In all his long and eventful life, passed amid peril, it is doubtful if the trapper had ever been in a wilder scene. The rapids were ahead and the fire behind and on either side. The great mass of flame had not yet rolled abreast the boat, but the blazing brands were already falling in advance. It was not a moment to hesitate; nor was he a man to falter when action was called for.

By this time the boat had come nigh the upper rift of the rapids, and the motion of the downward suction was beginning to tell on its progress. The trapper shipped his oars and, lifting his paddle, placed himself in a kneeling posture, gazing down stream. The fire was almost upon them, and the smoke too dense for sight. But pressing as was the emergency, neither man touched his paddle to the water, but let the boat go down with the quickening current to the verge of the rapids, where the sharp dip of the decline would send it flying.

"This be an onsartin ventur', Henry," cried the trapper, shouting to his comrade from the smoke that now made it impossible for the young man, even at only the boat's length, to see his person, "this be an onsartin ventur', and the Lord only knows how it will eend. Ye know the waters as well as I do; and ye know the p'ints where things must be did right. We'll beat the smoke arter we make the fust dip and git out of the thickest of it in the fust half of the distance, onless somethin' happens. Let her go with the current, boy, ontil yer sight comes to ye, for the current knows where it's goin', and that's more than a mortal can tell in this infarnal smoke. Here we gó, boy!"

shouted the old man as the boat balanced in its perilous flight on the sharp edge of the uppermost rift. "Here we go, boy!" he shouted out of the smoke and the rush of waters, "it's hotter than tophet where we be and it matters mighty leetle what meets us below."

II.

To those who have had no experience in running rapids, no adequate conception can be given touching what can with truth be called one of the most exciting experiences that man can pass through. The very velocity with which the flight is made is enough of itself to make the sensation startling. The skill which is required on the part of the boatman is of the finest order. Eye and hand and readiest wit must work in swift connection. Some who read these lines perhaps have — shall we say? — enjoyed the sensation which we have always found impossible to describe in words. These, at least, will appreciate the difficulty of our task, and also the peril which surrounded the trapper and his companion.

The first flight down which the boat glanced was a long one. The river bed sloped away in a straight direction for nigh on to fifty rods, and at an angle so steep that the water, although the bottom was rough, fairly flattened itself as it ran; and the channel where the current was the deepest gave forth a serpentine sound as it whizzed downward. The smoke which hung heavily over the stretch from shore to shore, was too dense for the eye to penetrate a yard. Amid the smoke sparks floated, and brands, crackling as they fell, plunged through it into the steaming water. Guidance of the frail craft was, as the trapper had predicted, out of the question; the two men could only keep their position as they went streaming downward. They kept their seats like statues, knowing well that their safety lay in allowing their light shell to follow without the least interruption the prevalent pressure of the swift current.

Half down the flight the volume of smoke was parted, by some freak of the wind, from shore to shore, and for a couple of rods they saw the water, the blazing banks, the fiery treetops, and each other. The trapper turned his face, blackened and stained by the grimy cinders, toward his companion and gave one glance, in which humor and excitement were equally mingled. His mouth was opened, but the words were lost in the roar of the flame and the rush of the water. He had barely time to toss a hand upward, as if by a gesture he would make good the impossibility of speech, before face and hand alike faded from Herbert's eyes as the boat plunged again into the smoke.

The next instant the boat launched down

the final pitch of the declivity and shot far out into the smooth water that eddied in a huge circle in the pool below. The smoke was at this point less compact; for through it the blazing pines on either shore flamed partially into view.

"It's the devil's own work, boy, for sartin," cried the trapper, "and the fool or the knave that started the fire oughter be toasted. I trust the pups will be reasonable and come down with the current. Has the fire teched ye anywhere?"

"Not much," answered Herbert. "A brand struck me on the shoulder and opened a hole in my shirt, — that is all. How do you feel?"

"Fried, boy; yis, actally fried. Ef this infarnal heat lasts I'll be ready to turn afore we reach the second bend."

"How goes the stream below?" asked Herbert.

"All clear for a while," answered the trapper, "all clear for a while. Put yer strength into the paddle till we come to the varge below, for the fire be runnin' fast, and it's agin reason for a mortal to stand this heat long."

"Shall we run out of the smoke at the next flight?" asked Herbert.

"I think so, boy, I think so," answered the trapper, "the maples grow to the banks at the foot of the next dip, and it isn't in the natur' of hard wood to make smoke like a balsam."

He would have said more, but his companion had nodded to him as he had ended the sentence, for they had come to the last flight of the rapids, and the great pool lay glimmering through the branches of the trees below.

The old man knew what was meant and said: "I know it, boy, I know it. Take the east run, for the water be deeper that way, and the boat sets deep. I won't trouble ye, for ye know the way. Lord! how the water biles! Now's yer time, boy, — to the right with ye! to the right! Sweep her round and let her go!"

Away and downward swept the boat. The strong eddies caught it, but the controlling paddle was stronger than the eddies, and kept it to the line of its safest descent. Past rocks that stood in mid current, against which the swift-going water beat and dashed, — past mossy banks and shadowed curves where the great eddies whirled — down over miniature falls into the bubbles and froth the light craft swept, and with a final plunge and leap jumped the last cascade, and, darting out into the great basin, ran shoreward.

It touched the beach, and the trapper and Herbert rose to their feet; but for a moment neither stirred, for in front of them, not thirty feet away, at the line where the sand and the green mosses met, and looking directly at them, *stood a man and a girl!*

. . . .

WHO WAS HE? The two men asked this question a thousand times mentally in the next two months, and once afterward they asked it aloud, as they looked into each other's eyes across a grave. But to the question, whether spoken or silent, no answer ever came.

The world has its enigmas, and he was one.

Amid the jabbering crowd we chaff and chatter with, we meet occasionally a man who never chaffs nor chatters, — a man who sees all things: perhaps because of this, suffers all things, but says nothing at all. The sphinxes are still extant. The old time ones were of stone and bronze; the modern ones are of flesh and blood: that's all the difference. Nay, not quite all; for the secrets that the ancients held smothered within the folds of their stony silence were only such as nature revealed to them from her desert posts, — the secrets of sunrises and starry nights, and simooms that swept the sandy plain, and of civilizations the murmurs of whose rising, and the crash of whose sudden overthrow, they needs must hear. But the secrets that men hear to-day, and by hearing of which are made silent, are the secrets of lives being lived, of hearts being broken, of intentions so noble and failures so bitter as to make men sceptical whether God keeps watch over the passing events on the earth.

Was he young? No. Was he old? No, again. How old was he? Forty, perhaps: it may be fifty. The two men who stood looking at him never thought of his age, neither then nor afterward; never thought whether he was old or young. There are people who have no age to those who know them. Is it because their bodies so little represent them? A friend has been away — for years. He returns; enters your room; you shake his hand heartily in welcome. And then you stand off and look at him. You look at his hair, and note the gray in it — at the wrinkles in his face — the dozen and one marks that denote change — and say, "you've grown old, old boy;" and so we judge most men, and so they should be judged. Why? Because they are not great and strong and soul-large enough to dwarf their bodies out of sight and dwindle them into insignificance.

But now and then you meet one whose mind represents him, whose soul is so gloriously finished that, as in the case of a great painting, you do not think of the frame around it, nor take notice of it at all. He is so strong vitally; so great in living force — in vital energies — in moving and persuading power — that he is to you like an immense, endless, all-conquering Life, wholly independent of his embodiment, who might exist in any form, — angel, archangel, spirit, winged or wingless, supernal or infernal, and still, in all forms, in all places, in all moral states would remain true to himself and be the same. There are some, I say, who are like this, — who are not of the earth, earthy, nor of the body, but of the spirit, whether good or bad, spiritual: angel or demon, always.

Do you know one such? No? Perhaps not, for they are rare, very rare. But some such there are, and if you know one, or one like to such a one, I ask you if you do not think of him as I have said? Body! what is a body to such a man? what is a formation of clay, deftly mingled in its chemistry round about such an indomitable indwelling spirit? Does the old rain-sodden nest photograph the bird, the swiftness and glory of whose wings lived in it once? What is age to such a one? What has he to do with the passing of years? Such a one is young and old both, from the beginning of his career forever onward. He has the freshness of youth, the strength of manhood, and the sagacity of age, fixed permanently in his structure, as nature fixes her colors in the fibre of the ash and the oak. Such have no age. How silly to ask how old he is? If you ask me, I should answer, *Who can tell?* Their earthly parents say they were born on such and such dates. Were they? or had they lived as Mary's Son had, ages before they took — for God's wise purpose — flesh? who can tell?

"*Heresy?*" I'm not writing a sermon, I am writing a story, and I seek to make my readers think. That would not be essential if I were sermonizing. Good people don't want that kind of preaching.

But to return. Was he young? Was he old? Neither then nor ever after did Herbert and the trapper think of him as having age; and yet he was with them, and his body had all the marks which reveal to the noticing eye the measure of man's days. This is the young man's description of him: —

"'Tall, straight, and well-formed; large in size, but shapely, hair, brown, with gray in it; in all the face a look of great power, reserved, but ready to act; eyes of changeable color, that took the shade of the emotion that chanced to come and look out of them: when unoccupied, cold, gray, and meaningless as a window-pane behind which no face is; and over all the countenance the look of great gravity, divided but by the slightest line from sadness."

So Herbert described him; but he always

used to add: "Remember, this was only his body, and *therefore no description at all.*"

The girl? Why, certainly, you shall know of her, and from the same authority:—

"The girl that was with this strange man was not a girl merely but both girl and woman; for she was at that age when the sweet simplicity of the one, and the full charm of the other, come into union, and for a time, at least, stand in attractive alliance. She was of medium height, and perfectly formed. Her hair was brown, as were her eyes, that were large and mild of look; and over all her face was such an expression of gentleness and peace as I never saw on any other woman's face, and she loved the man with so great a love that it made her life and took it both."

. . . .

For a moment Herbert and the trapper stood looking at the man and the girl, who were standing on the edge of the beach, looking silently at them; and then the trapper said, still standing in the boat, —

"We would not have run agin ye so sudden-like had we seed ye, friend; and ef our company be not pleasant to ye, we will move on, and camp on some clump furder down," and the old man placed his paddle against the beach as if he would breast the boat out into the pool.

"I beg you not to do so," answered the man on the beach; "you have as good a right to this camp-ground as we, and I dare say a better one, as we are but strangers to the woods; while you, old man, look as if you had made them your home for years."

"Ye speak the truth, friend," replied the trapper. "Yis, the woods be my home; and ef livin' in 'em gives man a right, few would gainsay my claim. Yis, it's thirty years agone sence I hefted the fust trout from this pool, and briled him on the bank there, — and a toothsome supper he made for me, too. Lord-a-massy, boy," exclaimed the old man, half turning toward his companion, "what a thing memory be! Thirty year! — and I've seed some wanderin' sence then, — but I remember as though I'd eat him last night jest how that trout tasted. You're sartin, friend, that we won't distarb ye ef we come ashore."

"No, no, old man," answered the other; "come ashore, — you and your companion. Our camp is the other side of the balsam thicket, there, and after you have built your own, we will come down and pass an hour with you, unless we should disturb you in your occupation or your pleasure."

"I be a man of the woods, as ye see," replied the trapper, "and Henry, here, be my companion; and though his home be in the city, he has consorted with me so much that he's fallen into my habits, — though it should be said to his credit that the Lord gin him nateral gifts in that direction; and when we be roamin', we take but leetle with us, and our camps be quickly made. No, no; we will have leetle to offer ye and the lady, but ef, when the sun darkens back of the mountin there, ye will honor an old man by yer comin', ye shall taste some venison that's waited three days for the mouth, and is tender, as it should be. And ef the pool here will make its name good, ye shall have a trout cooked as the hunter cooks it when the fire is hot and the wet moss plenty."

"We will certainly come," answered the man. "I came into the woods to avoid men, not to meet them; but your face is honest and open as the day, old man; and your head is white as is the head of wisdom. I shall be glad to talk with you, and I doubt not your companion is as educated as you are knowing."

"I've seed the comin' and goin' of seventy year sence I've been on the arth," answered the trapper, stroking his head with the peculiar motion of the aged when speaking of their age reflectively; "and much have I seed of the passions of my kind, and many be the lessons that natur' has larnt me; and ef the convarse of an old man who has lived leetle in the clearin's would be pleasant to ye, yer çomin' will be welcome. — Yis, yis, boy; I seed it. Ye had better j'int yer rod, and I will start a fire. Ye know the size ye want, and ye'll find 'em out there where the bubbles make the letter S."

The two strangers retired toward their own camp; and our friends set about their several tasks. Herbert proceeded to joint his rod, and the trapper to make a rude fire-place from the stones that lined the bank at the water's edge.

The preparations for the forthcoming repast went forward rapidly. The pool kept its reputation good, and yielded abundantly to the solicitation of Herbert's flies. The trout were large and in excellent condition, and were quickly made ready for the trapper's treatment. A large piece of bark, peeled from a giant spruce standing near, and laid upon the ground, served for the table, — against the dark bark of which the tin dishes freshly scoured in the sand of the beach gleamed brightly. The venison and trout were cooked as only one accustomed to the woods can do it, and the trapper contemplated the work of his skill with pleased complacency. At each plate Herbert had placed a bunch of checkerberries, and a small bouquet of small but exceedingly fragrant flowers adorned the centre of the bark table.

At this moment the man and girl drew near.

"I trust," said the man, as they approached, "that we have not kept you waiting by our tardiness?"

"Yer comin' be true to a minit," answered the trapper, glancing up at the western mountain, the top of whose pines the lower edge of the sun had just touched. "The meat be ready. We sartinly can't boast of the bark or the dishes," he continued, "but the victals be as good as natur allows, and yer welcome be hearty."

"We could ask no more," said the man courteously, "and one might almost think that the hand of a woman had adorned the table."

"The posies be the boy's doin'," replied the trapper, glancing at Herbert, "he has a likin' for their color and smell, and I never knowed him to eat without a green sprig or a bunch of bright moss or some sech thing on the bark."

"I am sure I do not like them any better than you do," answered Herbert, smiling, and looking pleasantly into the old man's face.

"They be of the Lord's makin'," responded the trapper. "They be of the Lord's makin', and it be fit that mortals should love 'em, as I conceit. I've lived a good deal alone," he continued, "but I never lived in a cabin yit that didn't have a few leetle flowers, or a tuft of grass, or a speck of green somewhere about it. They sort of make company for a man in the winter evenin's, and keep his thoughts in cheerful directions."

"Your sentiments do honor to your nature," responded the other; "and I am glad to meet with one of your age, who, having lived among the beauties of Nature, has not allowed them to become commonplace and unworthy of notice. Many in the cities show less refinement."

"I conceit it's a good deal in the breedin'," answered the trapper. "There be some that don't know good from evil in Natur', — leastwise, they don't seem to have any eyes to note the difference; and what isn't born in a man or a dog you can't edicate into him. The breedin' settles more p'ints than the missioners dream, as I jedge. But, come, friends, the victals be coolin', and the mouth loves a warm morsel."

"I am certain," said the man, as they were partaking of the repast, "that I never tasted a piece of venison so finely flavored before."

"I've cooked the meat for nigh on to sixty year," answered the trapper, "and have larnt not to spile the sweetness of natur' by overdoin' it. It's a quick aim that brings the buck to the camp, and a quick fire that puts the steak on to the plate ready for the mouth. — I trust, lady, that ye enjoy the victals?"

"I do, indeed," answered the girl; "and if the cooking were less perfect I should count this as a feast."

"Yis, yis; I understand ye," answered the old man. "The sound of the tumblin' water be pleasant, and the eye eats with the mouth," and he glanced at the green woods that stretched away, and the brightly-colored clouds that hung like fleece of gold in the western sky.

"The barbarian eats from a trough," remarked Herbert; "civilize him, and he erects a table; and as you add to his refinement, he adorns that table until the furniture of it magnifies the feast, and the guests think more of the beauty of the adornments than of the food they swallow."

And so with pleasant converse the meal progressed. Soon the sun declined, and darkness began to thicken in the pines. The table was moved to one side, the dishes cleansed, and the fire lighted for the evening. With the darkness silence had fallen on the group, — not that silence which is awkward and oppressive, or which comes from lack of thought, but that fine silence rather which is only the thin shadow of the reflective mood, and because the thought is inward and overfull.

And so the four sat in silence by the fire.

Above, a few great stars shone warmly. Here and there the rapids flashed white through the gloom. From a huge pine on the other side of the pool a horned owl challenged the darkness with his ponderous call.

Suddenly the man broke the silence, — broke it with a question which led to a remarkable conversation, and a tragical result. And the question was this: —

"Friends, answer me this question: *If a man take a life, should he give his own life in atonement for the dreadful deed?*"

III.

"*If a man take a life, should he give his own life in atonement for the dreadful deed?*"

Such was the question that the man asked. He was looking at the trapper at the time, — looking at him steadily; but the sound of his voice as he put the question did not seem to give personal direction to the solemn interrogation; it seemed rather the echo of a reflection, as if his own mind in its communings had come upon the terrible question, and the words, without volition of his own, which framed it into speech, had passed out of his mouth.

He was looking at the trapper, as we said, and the trapper was looking into the fire, — the light of which, that came and went in flashes, brought distinctly out the settled gravity of the features, and the rugged but grand proportions of the head. There is no better light in which to see an old man's face than the fitful firelight; and no better background than that which the darkness makes.

One would have thought that the interrogation was not heard, for on the trapper's face there showed no line of change. The girl remained looking steadfastly into the face of the questioner, and Herbert made no response.

"I asked you a question, old trapper," said the man; "a question which reaches to the depths of human responsibility, and points to the heights of human sacrifice. In the old days, the wisdom of the world was with those who lived with Nature. Your head is white, and you tell me you have lived in the woods since you were a boy. You have seen war; have stood in battle; have slain your man, and made many graves of those you have slain. Have you wisdom? Are you able to answer the question I have asked you?"

"I have, as ye say," answered the trapper, "ben in wars. I've stood in battle; I've slain men; I've buried those I have slain; I know what it is to take a human creetur's life, and I think I know where the right to do the deed stops and where it begins."

"Where does it begin?" asked the man; "where does the right to take human life begin?"

The words came forth slowly and heavy-weighted with meaning. It was evident that the question which the man asked was not asked as a theorist interrogates, but as one puts a question that has personal application to himself. The trapper felt this. He looked into the man's face, and studied his countenance a moment; noted the breadth of the brow, the large, deep-set eyes, the fine curvature of the chin and cheek; saw the beauty and splendor of it; saw what some might not have seen, — both the beauty of its peaceful mood and the terribleness of the wrath that might surge out of it, — saw all this, and without answering the question, said simply, —

"You have killed a man."

The stranger looked steadily back into the trapper's face, and answered as simply, —

"Yes, I am a murderer."

Herbert started a trifle. The girl gave a slight exclamation, and lifted her hand as if in protest. The trapper alone made reply, —

"Ye sartinly don't look like a murderer, friend."

"He is none! he is none!" exclaimed the girl. "He had provocation, old man! he had provocation!" and then she turned toward the man, and said: "Why will you say such things? Why will you condemn yourself wrongly? Why do you brood over a deed done in wrath, and under the strain that few might resist, as if it had been done in cool blood, and with a murderer's malice and forethought of evil?"

The man listened to her gravely, with a kind of considerate patience in the look of his face;

waited a moment, when she had finished, as one might wait from the habit of politeness, and then without answering her, said, —

"You have not answered my question, old trapper."

"I can't answer it, — I sartinly can't answer it, friend, onless I know the sarcumstances of the killin'; for there be killin' that is right and there be killin' that is wrong, and onless I know the sarcumstances of the killin', my words would be like the words of a boy that talks in council without knowing what he is talkin'. Ef ye killed a man, how did ye kill him?"

"I killed him face to face," answered the man. He paused a moment, and then repeated, "face to face."

"Why did ye kill him?" asked the trapper. "Had he done ye wrong?"

"He was my friend," said the man, "my friend, true and tried."

"Had he did ye a wrong?" persisted the trapper.

"What is wrong?" asked the man. "I can't tell whether he had done me wrong or nay. I only know he had crossed my purpose, — stopped me from doing what I had set my heart on doing; and what I set my heart on doing, old man, *I do*." And the man's eyes darkened under the abundant brow, and the face tightened and contracted as a rope when a strain is upon it. "The man came between me and my purpose," he added, "he stood up and faced me, and said I should not do what I purposed to do, and should not have what I had sworn to have; and I killed him where he stood."

It was astonishing how quietly the words were said, considering the tremendous energy of will which was charged into and through their quietness.

"He had no right to do it," said the girl; "he had no right to do it. It was none of his business, and you know it wasn't." And she spoke apparently to the man, "Oh, sir, why do you not tell them that he was an intermeddler, and meddled with what was none of his business, — kindled your rage by his meddling, and that you slew him in your rage, thoughtlessly, unintentionally? Why do you not tell them these things?"

The man listened to her again, politely. There was a look of grave courtesy in his eye, as he half turned his face and looked upon her as she was speaking; but beyond this there was no recognition that he heard her. When she had finished, he turned his face again toward the trapper, and said, —

"Old trapper, you have not answered my question. Has a man a right to take life?"

"Sartinly," answered the trapper.
"How?" asked the man.
"In war," answered the trapper.
"In any other way?" queried the man.
"Yis, — in self-defence."
"Any other cause?" persisted the stranger.
"Not as a rule," answered the trapper.

After this there was a silence. The girl's head dropped into her two palms, and for an instant her frame shook as one contesting the passage of a strong feeling that insists on expression. The three men made no motion, but sat silently gazing into the fire.

For several minutes the silence lasted. There are two living that will never forget that silence. Then the man lifted his face, and said, —

"Old trapper, have you ever known remorse?"

"I can't say I ever did," answered the trapper; "though I've felt a leetle oneasy arter dealin' with the thievin' vagabonds whose tracks I've found on the line of my traps. It has seemed to me, sometimes in the evenin', in thinkin' the matter over, that perhaps a leetle less bullet and a leetle more scriptur' might have did jest as well. But a man is apt to be a leetle ha'sh in his anger; and I have an idee that the Lord makes some allowance for a man's doin' when he's a good deal r'iled. That's where the marcy comes in. Yis; that's where the marcy comes in; isn't it, boy?" and the old man looked at Herbert.

"There is certainly where we need the mercy to come in," answered Herbert; "but it were better that we acted so that mercy need not be shown."

The man listened to Herbert's reply with an expression of strong assent on his countenance; then he turned to the trapper, —

"You say, old man, that you never knew remorse. Happy has your life been because of it; and happy shall your life be to its close. I have known remorse. It is a fearful knowledge, — as fearful as the knowledge of hell. Woe to the man that does an evil deed. That instant he is doomed, — doomed to anguish. His divinity punishes him. Within his bosom the great tribunal is instantly set up. The judge takes his seat. The witnesses are summoned; and the whole universe swarms to the trial. His memory is a torment; and all the forces of his mind suddenly concentrate in memory, — the memory of one deed, or of many deeds, even as his sin has been sole or manifold. What torment, old man, is like the torment of one whose memory is confined wholly to his evil deeds!"

No one made any reply. The anguish of the man's speech made response impossible.

"Before I did the deed," he continued, after a pause, "my memory took knowledge of all sweet things; of all dear faces I had ever seen; of all generous and blessed deeds I had ever done. But after that I could remember but one thing, — the murder; only one face, — the face of him I killed; and all my life, and the glory of it, was thrown into black eclipse by that one terrible act. Before I did the deed Nature was a joy to me, but now in every star I see his countenance looking down upon me. In every flower I see his still, cold face. The winds bear to me his voice. The water of those rapids" — and the man stretched his hand out toward the flowing river — "sounds to me like the rattle in his throat as he lay dying. How shall I find release, old man? How quit myself of this terrible curse?" and the man's words ended in a groan.

"The marcy of the Lord be great," replied the trapper; "greater than any deed of guilt did by mortal; great enough to cover you, friend, and your misdoin', as a mother covers the error of her child with her forgiveness."

"I know the mercy of the Lord is great," answered the man; "I know His forgiveness covers all; but the old law, — old as the world, — old as guilt and justice, — the law of life for life, and blood for blood, has never been repealed. And this is the one comfort left for the noble: that, however great the guilt, however wicked the deed, the atonement can be as great as the sin. He who dies pays all debts. He who has sent one to the grave, and goes to the grave voluntarily, goes into the arms of mercy. I know not where else, with all his searching, man may surely find it."

Again there was silence. Above, the stars shone warmly through the dusky gloom. The rapids roared, falling hoarsely through the darkness. A moaning ran along the pine-tops; the firelight flamed and flickered, and the flames flashed the four faces into sight that were grouped around the brands. At length the trapper said, —

"What is it ye have in yer heart to do, friend?"

"1 took a life," answered the man, "I must give a life in return. I took a life, and my life is forfeited. This is my condemnation, and I pronounce it on myself. My judge is not above; my judge is within. In this the world finds protection, and in this the sinner finds release from sin. There is no other way; at least, no other way so perfect. One man was great enough to die for the sins of others. They who would rise to the level of his life must be great enough to lay down their life for their own sins. This is justice; and out of such true justice blooms the perfect mercy." To this the man added thoughtfully, "there is but one objection."

"What is the objection?" asked Herbert. "What is the objection, if one be great enough to make so great a sacrifice?"

"The objection," answered the man, "is found in this: it is so deep a sin to kill; it is so easy a thing to die, — for what is death? The ignorant dread it because they do not analyze it; their lack of thoughtfulness makes them cowardly : for death is going out of bondage into liberty. He who passes through the dark gate finds himself, when he has passed, standing in the cloudless sunshine. In dying, the sorrowful become glad; the small become greater; and if they die rightly, the sinful become sinless. If a great motive prompts us to death, it is the perfect regeneration. Entering thus the new life, man is born anew. And so in punishment the great law of mercy stands revealed, and sin leads up to sinlessness. In such travail of soul, he who suffers through suffering is satisfied."

"It is sublime philosophy," exclaimed Herbert, "but few are great enough to practise it."

"Rather, sir," exclaimed the man, "few are

knowing enough to accept it. The eyes of men, through their ignorance, are blinded by fear, and they see not the delivering gates though they stand facing the open passage."

" Life is sweet."

The words fell from the lips of Herbert as if they spoke themselves.

" To the innocent, life is sweet," answered the man ; " but to the guilty, life is bitterness. The world was not made for the guilty. The beauties and glories of it were not for them. The universe is not sustained for them. Only for the good do things exist. The breasts of life are full; but their nourishment is not for guilty lips to draw. I have seen the time when life was sweet. I have lived to see the time when life is bitter. Through death I go out of bitterness into sweetness. This is the mercy that is unto all, and which all can take, — take freely. Some get it through another, — all might get it through themselves."

" It is a violent deed to kill one's self," said the trapper.

" You mistake," answered the man; "there is a coarse, rude way: there is a fine and noble way. 'I have power,' said the Man, 'to lay down my life, and I have power to take it again.' Do you not think, old trapper, that a man can die when he wills ? "

"I don't understand ye," answered the trapper.

"The soul rules the body," replied the stranger. "The soul is not bound to the body; it lives in it as a man lives in his house. My body is only my environment. I can quit it at will. I can go out of it."

"Do you mean to say," asked Herbert, "that we can leave our bodies through determination of purpose and mental decision?"

"There have been such cases," answered the man, "and such cases there might be continually. If the relations between the soul and body are recognized, and the supreme authority of the one over the other allowed full action, the soul can do any thing it pleases. It can come and it can go. This is my faith."

While the foregoing conversation was being conducted, the girl had remained silent. Herbert sat opposite to her; and as the firelight flamed her face into sight, he could but note the expression of it. The look of her face was that of one who was listening to what she had heard before, — perhaps many times before, — and which, upon the hearing, she had combated and was determined to continue to combat. And at this point she suddenly spoke up, —

"I think, sir," — and she lifted her eyes to the face of the man, — "that the living should live for the living rather than die for the dead; for the dead have no wants, neither of the body nor of the heart, — neither of the mind nor the soul; or, if they want, God feeds them. But the living want, and crave, and have deep needs, and God feeds them not at all unless through us who live; and it is our duty to do, and not to die."

The words were clearly and slowly spoken, — spoken in a quiet but determined tone. The old trapper raised his face and looked at the girl, as if surprised at the wisdom of her speech. Herbert was already looking at her. The man slowly turned his face towards her, and said, —

"Mary, we have argued that point before."

The tone in which he spoke was not one of rebuke, and yet it conveyed the idea that the point was settled and was not to be re-opened. The girl waited a moment respectfully, as if she felt profound deference for the other's character, and would not willingly oppose his wish, and then she said, —

"I know, sir, we have discussed it before; but it is not settled, and never can be settled; for it sets in comparison the value of two lives, — the one that was and the one that is; and I say that there are lives — of which yours is one — that belong to others, and cannot be disposed of as if they were a selfish thing. And life is truer atonement for sin than death. You owe more than one debt; and you have no right to pay the one, however great it is, if by the paying of that you leave the others unpaid."

"Friend," said the trapper, "the girl speaks wisdom; leastwise she brings matter into the council which men of gravity should not overlook. The livin' sartinly have claims. What can you say to her speech?"

For a moment the man made no reply, and then he said, —

"My philosophy is based upon a sentiment, — a sentiment born of conscience, — and conscience makes duty for us all. There is no reasoning against conscience. It is the voice of God; the only God we have. My conscience tells me that there is but one atonement that I can make. There is no election. I must do it."

"What good," said Herbert, addressing the man, "what good will you do by dying?"

"I shall satisfy myself," said the man.

"And what right have you, to satisfy yourself in such a matter?" exclaimed the girl. "What right have any of us to satisfy ourselves? What right have we to be selfish in our death any more than in our life? Oh, sir, if you saw rightly, you would see that you had no right to satisfy yourself in this dreadful way. You should satisfy others. They need you even as the poor need the rich; as the weak need the strong; as those who are prone, because they cannot lift themselves, need one who is strong enough to lift them. It is not heroic to die, unless the full object of life is met by the dying. It is heroic to live, because it is harder than dying. Even death dedicated to atonement can be a greater sin than the deed which one would atone."

"I know not how the girl has such wisdom," said the trapper, "for she be young; and yit she sartinly seems to me to have the right of it. I know not who ye be, nor how many look to ye for help; but ef ye be one that can help, and there be many that need yer help, I sartinly conceit that ye should live, — live to help 'em."

"You say right! You say right, old man!" exclaimed the girl. "His life is not a common life. It represents such power and faculty and opportunity, and I may say such devotion to the many, that it does not belong to him, and may not therefore be disposed of as if he owned it himself and had the right to do with it as he pleased."

"I do not say," answered the man, "that I own my life. I say rather that I do not own it. I owe it. There are debts you cannot pay by life. The laws of the whole world recognize this; nor do we do by living the greatest service. He who dies to uphold a righteous principle fulfils all righteousness. He who gives away a life in atonement for a life taken makes all life more sacred; and so he serves the living beyond all other service he might do. She looks at individuals; I observe principles. She contemplates only the present; I forecast the future needs of man. Moreover, the highest service one can do man is to serve himself in the highest manner. He who ministers to his own sense of justice strengthens the judicial sense of the world. Men overvalue life when they suppose that there is nothing better. To teach them that there is something better, — to impress them by some signal event that there is something higher and nobler than mere living, — is to fulfil all benevolence to their souls. How many the Saviour could feed and heal and bless by avoiding Calvary! and yet he did not avoid it. He showed the object of life, which is service. I trust I have not wholly failed to show men that. He then showed the highest object of dying, which is service. Why should I not imitate him? Why should I not be a law unto myself, and bear the penalty voluntarily?"

The man rose to his feet as he concluded, and looking at the trapper and Herbert said, —

"Gentlemen, I thank you for your hospitality and your courtesy," — and turning to the girl, he said, "Mary, we will talk this matter over more fully by ourselves."

And then he bowed to the group and turned away.

IV.

Long after the man and the girl had departed, the trapper and Herbert sat by their campfire discussing the question which their guest had propounded. Their conversation was grave and deliberate, as became the theme; and they united in the opinion that if the deed had been done in anger elicited by a provocation, the man should give himself the favor which the law even would allow under similar circumstances.

"I tell ye, Herbert," said the trapper, "the girl said the man had cause, — leastwise, that the man whom he struck worried him to it; and that the blow was given in anger. Now hot blood is hot blood, and cold blood is cold blood, and ef a man kill another man in cold blood it be murder, — the law says so, and what is better, natur' says so; — but ef a man kill another man in his anger, when his blood is up and he is strongly provoked to it, the law says there be a difference, and what be better, natur' says there be a difference, and it isn't murder. And I conceit, that the girl be right, and that the man has no right in natur', or law either, to murder himself because in his anger he murdered another man. And besides," continued the old man, after a moment's pause, during which he had evidently made an effort at memory, "ef there be any wrath in the case it belongs to the Lord, and not to man. Ye may recall the varse, Henry."

"'*Vengeance is mine, I will repay, saith the Lord.*'" Such was the quotation Herbert made.

"Sartinly, sartinly," answered the trapper; "that is it. Vengeance is the Lord's, and he is the only one that can handle it rightly; and the man had better leave it to the Lord."

For several moments Herbert made no reply; and then, as if speaking to himself more than his companion, he said, —

"How the girl loves him!"

"Ye've hit it, Henry," answered the trapper, promptly. "Yis; ye've hit it in the centre. I noted her face: the look in her eyes, and the arnestness of her voice; and there is no doubt about the matter of the lovin'. She is one of the quiet kind, boy; and she has got the faculty of listenin' a long time, — which isn't nateral to a woman. But when she speaks, ye can see what she is. She has a quiet face, but a detarmined sperit. I've seed several of the same sort, — seed them afore the battle and arter the battle;

and I know what's in the heart of the girl. Yis; I know what's in the heart of the girl," and the old man looked at his comrade across the camp-fire.

The young man returned his gaze, and then said, quietly, —

"What is in the heart of the girl, John Norton?"

"Ef the man dies the girl dies too," answered the trapper, and stooping he pushed a brand into the centre of the fire.

"It is awful to think so," replied the young man; "it is awful to think that one so lovely should die so young, and die so miserable."

"She belongs to the kind that does sech things," answered the trapper. "But whether ye can call her dyin' miserable, I sartinly doubt; for there be some that can't die miserable owin' to their feelin's. And I've noted that them that die feelin' a sartin way die happy whenever they die; for death means one thing to one and another thing to another; and the heart that has lost all, is happy to go in sarch of it even ef it be along the trail that the sun never shines on."

And so the two men sat and talked, feeding the camp-fire with sticks occasionally as they talked. They wondered who the man was, and whence he came; wondered if he would change his views, and if the girl could win him over to a rational way of looking at the deed that had been done, and the true way to atone for it; wondered if they could not assist her in her loving task when the morning came; talked and wondered and planned, and at last wrapping their blankets around them, they laid down to sleep. The last words spoken being by the Trapper, and were these, —

"We will go over in the mornin', Herbert, and help the girl."

And then they slept.

. . . .

Beyond the balsam thicket, by another campfire, the girl and the man sat talking, — talking of the deed that had been done, and the atonement demanded, and of the great future beyond this present life; the future that stretches away endlessly, the future of peace to some, — perhaps to all, who knows? For there be some who think that this life has in it such forces of education, such enlightenment to the understanding, such quickening to the conscience, such ripening of character; and that through its experiences, its trials, and its griefs, come such graces to the souls of those that leave it, that when they pass they leave their worse self behind them, even as the germ leaves the shuck out of which it has sprouted, — leaves it in the dull, damp ground forever while it groweth up into the sunlight in which it finds perfection.

"Mary," said the man, "I have done with the past. My mind turns wholly toward the future. I see it as the shipwrecked sailor sees the land which, if he can but reach, he will not only be beyond the storm that wrecks him but beyond all storms forever. Companion of my joys, and companion of my grief, — companion in every thing but in my sin, — counsel with me, with your eyes turned ahead. You are innocent, and innocence is prophetic. What lies beyond this world, and the life men live in it? What of good waits for him who gives up this life bravely and penitently, and trusts himself to the decisions and the certainties of the great hereafter?"

"My master," said the girl, "it is not for me to teach you, — you who are so much greater than I, — you who have been gifted with faculties and powers that have lifted you above men. What can I say to you save to repeat what you have said to me?"

"Mary," he replied, "talk to me from out your heart, and not from out your mind. The prophecies that come to men from Heaven, Heaven has communicated through the emotions of the just and the good and the pure, and not through the perceptions. Tell me of the faith of your heart,— the heart which I know has been free of guile. Tell me of the great Hereafter, and what awaits me there."

"The Hereafter?" said the girl, and she lifted her eyes lovingly to the face of the man; "the Hereafter is the same as the Here, only larger: as things grown are larger than things ungrown. The Future is to the Present what the river is to the stream, what the stream is to the fountain: it is the flowing out and the flowing on, the widening and the deepening of what is."

"Is there no gap, no breakage, no chasm or gulf between the Here and the Hereafter?" asked the man.

"No," said the girl, "there is no gap nor chasm nor gulf, but continuity of progress and perfect sequence. The connections between the Known and the Unknown are perfect. The one does not end and the other begin. Time is the beginning of eternity; and the brief time that men call a day is only a fraction of endlessness."

"There is no end to life, then?" queried the man.

"End to life!" exclaimed the girl, "how can life end? Life changes its form, its embodiment, the location of its residence; but life is the breath of God, and when once breathed into the universe, and it has taken form and made for itself expression, who may annihilate it? who may take it out of existence? No, master, there is no end to life."

"It is a sublime faith," said the man, "and I have proclaimed it unto many; but few have been great enough to receive the doctrine as a verity. In theory they have received it; but their superstition has robbed them of its mighty consolations. But if we do not die, but only pass forward as men go out of a city's gate along a road that has no end, what fate befalls them? Does a change of nature come to them?"

"Only such as comes through growth," answered the girl.

"Shall I be just as I am when I have passed into the great future?" he asked.

"You will be the same," answered the girl, "only more abundantly yourself. We are all our life looking for ourselves," continued the girl, "and few, if any, find themselves until they die."

"I don't understand," said the man, "I know the Lord is speaking through you; for you are uttering truths so great that at the utterance they seem mysteries. Explain as the teacher explains to the child she is trying to teach."

"I mean," answered the girl, "that death is an enlightenment and a discovery. It will give us revelations of God because it will give us revelations of ourselves; for never do we find Him save as we find Him in His: and we are His. You will not know who and what you are until you get far enough ahead, my master, to look back upon yourself. We must go up and go on a long way before we know what we are now."

Here the conversation paused for a while, and nothing disturbed the profound silence but the roar of the rapids whose ceaseless sound swelled and sank in the silence like the waves of the sea. At length the man said, "Have you thought of the land ahead? Is it real? and where is it? and what the life lived there?"

"Why do you ask me such questions," answered the girl, "when you know that I have thought only as you have taught me to think, and am but repeating the faith I learned from your lips? Surely there is a land ahead, or rather many lands; lands and seas and blessed islands in the seas where the blessed live; and loves and lovers, and homes exquisitely and endlessly peaceful are there; and men who have grown nobler than they were here, and women far sweeter than their short life here might make them, live and love in the lands ahead."

The girl spoke low but earnestly; and her words sounded on the silent air like softly-breathed music, so much did her sweet self possess her words. And the man listened as men listen to music when it comes softly and sweetly to their ears.

"Mary," said the man, "you make the life ahead seem so sweet that I shrink from entering it, lest by so doing I escape the punishment for my sin I would fain inflict upon myself."

"Oh, master!" exclaimed the girl, "you do mistake; for though I do believe all I have said, and would trust myself to the far future as young eagles trust themselves to the warm air when they have grown equal to the joy of flight, yet the life of this earth is sweet, — so sweet when the heart is satisfied that one might fear to exchange it for another as one fears to part with what fully satisfies, even though the promise of more abundant things is sure as God. It is sweet to breathe the airs of the earth as health receives them. 'Tis sweet to live and love, and serve in loving, and find your happiness in giving it. 'Tis sweet to teach and guide men up and on to wider knowledge and nobler living, — to make them gentler and finer in their thoughts, and happier-hearted; and oh, my master, 'tis sweet to live with one you love; be unto him a new life daily, and see him grow in your growth, matching it, and so go on in that perfect companionship that the future may give to us as the highest fortune ; and having given, has given its best and all."

"You shall live," answered the man; "you shall live and have as you deserve, dear girl; and if I have taught you aught which, being known, has made or shall make your life on earth sweeter, take it as my legacy to you. I had thought to leave you something more, — perhaps something better; but that is past."

"I will not take your legacy and stay," answered the girl; "I will rather take it and go with you, that where you are I may be with you. You have promised nothing, and I want no promise. I have only asked one thing, and only one thing now do I ask, and that you will not hold from me, for I have earned it, — earned it by patient serving and by growth that you know came from you."

"What is it that you ask? tell me," replied the man, "for you shall have it if it be in the power of my giving."

"Companionship," answered the girl, — "the companionship of service. My mind must serve your mind; for only so may it find its growth for which it longs. You have led me from darkness to light; and into what future light you advance I must enter too. I love you as women love men; but I love you more than that. I love you for what you are separate from what you can ever be to me. I love you as a mind. I love you as a soul. I love you as a spirit. I love you with a purity, with an ambition, with a longing that men cannot interpret, and earthly relations cannot express; but which God understands, and which in his Heaven I know there must be a name for, and a connection that is known through all the social life of Heaven."

"It must not be," answered the man. "I admit your claim; but it must not be."

"Why must it not be?" asked the girl.

The man hesitated a moment, and then he said, —

"Because my future is uncertain; I dare not say what it will be."

"I care not what it is," answered the girl. "Whatever it is, that I share, — share because I cannot help it. It is not a question of condition, but of presence. With you I could bear all misery; yea, in the misery find happiness. Without you my heart could feel no joy throughout all eternity. Master, my master, I love you so!" and as she looked into the face of the man there came to her countenance the expression of utter devotion; and in her large eyes tears gathered, and, having formed, from them slowly fell.

The man groaned aloud, and said, —

"Alas! alas! My curse is doubled, being brought on thee."

"There is no curse on thee or me," she answered. "You were but mortal, and being sorely tempted, did a wicked deed. But no single deed can change the nature. You are the same great man, — great in your goodness as you are great in power, and my love too remains the same; nay, master, it is greater. You should stay and live, and make atonement by living; for you cannot live and not better men. You can do deeds that would wipe out the deadliest guilt. But if you will not stay; if to you it seems right to die, and if only through death your sense of justice can be met, and yourself find peace, then neither will I stay, but go, — go where thou goest. Yea; I will sink or rise with thee; go to this world or that, I care not which or where if only I may be with thee. And I pray thee not to think it hard for me to share thy journey. Why should I be left behind? and what might I have, thou being gone? What pleasure in all the world could I find, with thee out of it? I have no home: thy presence is my home. I have no kindred, and no loves await me anywhere. How could I have, loving thee, for in thee I have found father and mother, brother and sister, and all sweet relationships? And so whither thou goest, let me go; and where thou stayest, let me stay. Do not resist me, but be persuaded, and let me die with thee. So shall we, passing out of these mortal bodies in the self-same hour, be together still."

The man made no response; but sat silently gazing at her face. In a moment the girl moved softly to his side, and took his hand in hers; and so they sat together while the firelight died away, and the darkness enveloped them. But through the darkness the stars beamed mildly, as if they expressed the sweet mercy which the imaginations of men picture as throned above the azure in whose blue field they stand suspended.

What happened farther is known only to Him whose eyes see through all darkness, and to whom the night is as the day.

During the night the trapper started suddenly from his sleep. Was it a woman's cry he heard? Was it only such a sound as comes to us at times in dreams? He listened, but heard nothing save the monotonous murmur of the rapids, and the equally-steady movement of the night-breeze stirring through the pine-tops. He listened, and hearing nothing, lay down again, and slept.

The morning came, — came as brightly and cheerfully as if the world knew no sorrow, and the men and women in it had no griefs. The morning came; but before it came, a wing darker than the shadow of the night had passed over the woods; for when the Trapper and his companion visited the camp beyond the balsam thicket, they found the two lying side by side, — the girl's head on the bosom of the man, and her right hand lying gently in his; no mark of violence on their bodies; no instrument of death near; — lying as if they had fallen asleep, the man's countenance in grave repose, the girl's blessedly peaceful; — no name on either; no scrap of paper that might tell who they might be. Perhaps the man's faith was true. Perhaps the will has power to will itself, and all of life there is within us, out of the body. Be this as it may, the trapper and his companion only saw this: the unknown man in the prime of his strength lying dead under the pines, and the girl in her loveliness lying dead by his side.

Who were they?

www.ingramcontent.com/pod-product-compliance
Lightning Source LLC
Chambersburg PA
CBHW021830230426
43669CB00008B/927